The Encyclopedia of CARS

VOLUME ONE – Abarth to Buick

The Encyclopedia of CARS

VOLUME ONE – Abarth to Buick

Chelsea House Publishers

Philadelphia

Edited by Chris Horton
Foreword by Karl Ludvigsen

Published in 1998 by
Chelsea House Publishers
1974 Sproul Road, Suite 400
P.O. Box 914
Broomall, PA 19008-0914

Printed in Italy

**Library of Congress Cataloging-in-Publication
Data**
Encyclopedia of Cars/edited by Chris Horton: foreword
by Karl Ludvigsen.

     p.   cm.
    Includes indexes.
    ISBN 0-7910-4865-9 (vol. 1)
    ISBN 0-7910-4866-7 (vol. 2)
    ISBN 0-7910-4867-5 (vol. 3)
    ISBN 0-7910-4868-3 (vol. 4)
    ISBN 0-7910-4869-1 (vol. 5)
    ISBN 0-7910-4870-5 (vol. 6)
    ISBN 0-7910-4871-3 (vol. 7)
    ISBN 0-7910-4864-0 (set)

1. Automobiles–Encyclopedias. I. Horton, Chris.
TL9. E5233 1997   97-17890
629.222 03–DC21   CIP

Page 2: BMW 5 Series Touring
Page 3: Bugatti EB 110
Right: Bentley Brooklands R

Contents

Foreword

I think of the car as the 'seven-league boots' of the legend that first gave man the ability to cover huge distances with ease. Even the most basic motor vehicle offers tremendous powers of liberation. This creates a demand and a desire for cars that is, dare I say it, frankly gratifying to those of us who both love cars and eke out a living from their creation and use.

This powerful man/machine symbiosis no doubt accounts for the many cars that are named after their creators. Leafing through the seven volumes of **The Encyclopedia of Cars**, you will find these in by far the majority.

No decree exists stating that cars should be named for the men that brought them into being (and with no exception that I can recall they have indeed been men rather than women). Benz and Daimler, however, started the fashion early. That many others followed suit can be attributed as much to ego as to rationality.

To be sure, many of the creators gave their cars names that in retrospect are wonderful. Consider Chrysler, Cord and Duesenberg, for example, Ferrari too is resonant of ripping exhausts – even though the name is Italian for Smith.

As a joint effort, no car name surpasses the marriage of C.S. Rolls with Henry Royce. I remind myself that Rolls-Royce is hyphenated by the saying that Claude Johnson, the firm's indefatigable secretary, was the hyphen between Rolls and Royce.

Naming cars after their creators has continued to the present day. Among the more recent DeLorean and Honda had an advantage, in my opinion, in tonal resonance over Tucker and Bricklin.

The more prolific car creators created problems with their second-generation efforts that for the most part they neatly solved. Ransom E. Olds went on to build the REO after leaving the Oldsmobile behind at General Motors. Having given up the brand bearing his surname. Harry C. Stutz was less successful with the HCS.

August Horch tried a second time with Audi, the Latin word for his German surname: 'listen'. Only after leaving the company he founded, General Motors, was William C. Durant able to build a car in his own name. Some of the creators showed striking modesty. Either Cadillac or Lincoln could have been named after the Leland brothers that brought both marques to life. Although we are quite happy with Cisitalia, would Dusio not have been even more evocative?

Rarest, perhaps, have been the cars that bear first or given names. They range from the sublime (Mercedes) to the ridiculous (Henry J). Not to be forgotten is the Edsel, an inapt tribute to the member of the Ford family with the finest eye for design, or the Doretti, whose name was a variation upon Dorothy – an inspirer rather than a creator. Emil Jellinek was the entrepreneur who named the Daimler-build product after his daughter Mercedes. Herr Jellinek was less successful with his next such effort. The Austrian-built Maja was a fine car but not a survivor.

I am not among those who easily use Mercedes alone to describe the cars built by Daimler-Benz after the fusion of the two companies in 1926. My researches into the racing cars they built convinced me that the talents of the Benz men contributed as much or more to their successes than did those of the Daimler (Mercedes) engineers. I can only refer to the post-1926 marque as Mercedes-Benz.

Cars have also been given geographical place names, although the relevance of some is obscure. William Gunn, for example, is said to have found Lagonda on a map of Ohio, but I have not yet had the chance to confirm that in a gazetteer of that Midwestern American state.

The Hispano-Suiza marque honoured the conjoint Spanish and Swiss origins of those great cars and aero engines. Tatra and Steyr were named for Czech and Austrian regions respectively. Auburn is an Indiana city and Mercer a New Jersey county. And when the *Mayflower* landed at Plymouth Rock, another car marque was created (as well as a model name for Triumph).

As hood ornaments or mascot Plymouths once carried replicas of the *Mayflower* in full sail. Pontiacs flaunted the profile of the American Indian chief for whom the marque's town of manufacture was named. In the early 1950s, Pontiacs were among the most boring cars in America. Encumbered by their 'silver streaks' and Indian heads, they were relentlessly dull if worthy cars. This so frustrated the car stylists as G.M. that they argued that the Pontiac should be renamed. Instead, 'Bunkie' Knudsen changed the car – which went on to tremendous success.

Peculiarly European (with some exceptions mentioned earlier) has been the naming of cars with acronyms. Some are pronounced letter by letter, like Britain's AC, TVR, G.N., M.G. and H.R.G. and Germany's BMW, N.S.U. and D.K.W. Others are pronounced as words, like Daf, Fiat, SEAT, Saab and the Alfa that is paired with the surname of Nicola Romeo.

In a world awash with acronyms, especially in Europe, their use for car marques should hold great promise. Future framers of acronyms for cars may be interested in a suggestion: make them work as a mirror image so they will read properly when they are seen in the rear-view mirror of the car ahead. An example: MAXXAM. I am just full of bright ideas for car names. When I worked for Fiat we were seeking a better name for the Ritmo for the American market. I dared to suggest we call it the Fiat Berry. We could then say it was Berry economical, Berry lively and Berry practical. Blueberry and blackberry were just a few of the colours. As a secretary at Fiat aptly observed, a used car would be known as an Elderberry. I still think it's a berry good idea.

Other names that are in regular use must surely be leading candidates for use as car marques. I refer to names that on 16 weekends each year receive worldwide television exposure of incalculable value. Among them are Williams, Lola, Arrows, March and Brabham – the racing cars which have no road counterparts. Only McLaren, whose Gordon Murray has designed an exotic, high-tech supercar has seized the opportunity, although Renault launched the successful and sought after Clio Williams hot hatchback.

Incredibly, companies that have had access to evocative car marques have not hesitated to give them up. Rover Group, formerly Austin-Rover and now owned by BMW, let Morris and Austin wither on the car marque vine. First they neglected their nurturing. Next they expressed surprise that the names no longer had positive associations, a fact they discovered in their effort to relaunch M.G. as a separate marque. Throughout the 1980s the only sign of the M.G. octagon was on the sporty versions of Metros, Maestros and Montegos. Almost all association with proper sports cars had gone. Thankfully, the large amount of MGBs still running around meant that the public were forced to remember and the marque's relaunch was a success, but only following the launch of its second car, the MCF.

Such cavalier treatment of car marques will not serve in the future. Rather, car manufacturers need to take even more care in defining, positioning and communicating the characters and attributes of their brands. Many have started to do so, by strengthening the corporate image of their cars by reintroducing features for which their marques were famous. Rover Group, for example, reintroduced the traditional Rover grille in the early 1990s.

This need has arisen for several reasons. The 'commonization' of cars under the skin to save production costs will accelerate, under Ford 2000, for example, which aims to reduce the number of Ford car platforms by the year 2000, placing a greater burden on image communication.

Competition is intensifying in markets that are increasingly cluttered with 'manufactured' brands like Geo, Saturn, Acura, Lexus and Infiniti. Starting now, to meet the competition of the next century, the successful car makers will foster and, if needed, create marques that have the power to achieve fully global scope and impact.

A recent survey was made on the awareness and esteem accorded to 300 product brands, in Japan, the U.S.A. and Europe. Among the top 20 best known brands in those three markets, seven were automotive, eight if you count a tyre manufacturer.

The survey sharply contrasted attitudes to car marques in the U.S.A. and those in Europe. In the U.S.A. not one car marque, foreign or domestic, was among the 20 most powerful brands. In Europe, nine of the top twenty brands were automotive, with seven of them ranked in the top ten. One, Mercedes-Benz, was considered to be Europe's most potent brand name.

The strength in their images at home will serve the European auto makers well as they improve their efficiency and consolidate their powers to meet increasing competition from the rest of the world. 'What's in a name?' To William Shakespeare's question there is a ready answer from the motor industry: quite a lot.

1997 Ford Mustang GT

Abarth

Italy
1941-1971

Born in Yugoslavia of Italian parents, Carlo
Abarth moved to Italy at the end of World
War II, where he worked as an engineering
consultant and later became Porsche's
Italian representative.

The link with Porsche soon saw him
involved with Cisitalia. When Cisitalia failed,
Abarth took over the racing side and started
his own company in 1949. He soon started
building his own racing cars and later
branched out into producing aftermarket
tuning equipment, mainly for Fiat.

Abarth's first production car was the 204
Berlinetta, launched in 1950. It used a tuned
1100cc Fiat engine and Porsche-type torsion

Above: Abarth 750s at Le Mans in 1960

Below: Abarth 750 Zagato 'Double Bubble'

bar suspension. Despite its small engine it could top 110mph and even took Tazio Nuvolari to his last win.

In 1956 Abarth signed an agreement with Fiat which led to many of his cars being Fiat-based. The first was a tuned version of Fiat's tiny 600 saloon. Over the years he developed it into a highly specialized twin-cam Group 2 competition car. Meanwhile, the tuning

parts side of the business was booming and provided Abarth with a stable financial base to build even more of his exotic automotive creations.

A range of beautiful coupés soon followed, many of them becoming very successful competition cars, with incredible power outputs being squeezed from their tiny Fiat-based engines. The company continued to

modify Fiat saloons and later also built a Simca-based sports car in 1966.

The end came in 1971. Abarth's enthusiasm for racing cars had led him to neglect other areas of his business, putting him in deep financial trouble. Fiat came to the rescue and took over the tuning side of the business with Carlo Abarth as a technical consultant. The Abarth name did not die however, and went on to adorn many high-performance versions of Fiat models. Today, Abarth extras are limited to sporty steering wheels and wide alloy road wheels but the Abarth Scorpion logo can even be seen on Fiat's tiny Cinquecento.

Top: Abarth-Simca 1300, 1962
Left: 1959 Abarth 850 Allemano
Below: Abarth Spider by Zagato, 1959

AC

Great Britain
1904 to date

The origins of AC date back to 1904 when engineer John Weller and partner John Portwine, who owned a chain of butchers' shops, formed Autocars and Accessories Ltd.

This company, based in West Norwood, London, made cheap three-wheeled trade carriers from 1907 for businesses who could not afford a four-wheeled van. Customers included Selfridges and the Great Western Railway.

A passenger version called the AC Sociable was launched in 1908 and remained in production until 1914.

The company was renamed Auto Carriers in 1907 and moved to new premises at Thames Ditton, Surrey, four years later.

Production was halted by World War I, by which time the company had made a four-wheeled light car with 10hp French-built Fivet engine in limited numbers. S.F. Edge, from Napier, joined the board of AC in 1921 and was left in charge when Weller and Portwine resigned in 1922.

The company changed its name to AC Cars in 1922 and then AC (Acedes) in 1927. This company went into liquidation in 1929 and only the service department continued.

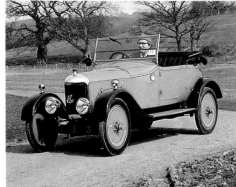

Above: 1923 AC Empire

Above: 1929 Acedes Magna

William and Charles Hurlock bought the factory in 1930 and William Hurlock was so pleased with a car assembled for him by the service manager that production began again.

Production was limited, however, and stopped during World War II.

The first post-war cars left the factory in 1947 and by 1951, with sales of AC's stylish but old-fashioned two-litre saloon falling, the company diversified into

Bottom: AC Sociable, built around 1910

Above: The AC Cobra was launched in 1962 with a 4.7-litre V8 engine and a top speed of 220km/h (138mph). American

tuner Carroll Shelby first produced the 427 cubic inch (7-litre) version in 1965. The Cobra is now reproduced as the AC Mk 4.

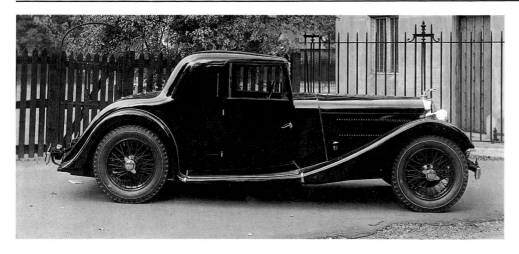

Above: Two-seater AC built around 1934   *Below: 1955 Ace (left) and 1956 Aceca*

Above: AC 428 Convertible launched 1966   *Right: 1984 AC Mk IV*

different fields, including three-wheeled invalid carriages.

The first of the sporting roadsters was the Ace – derived from a two-litre Bristol-engined competition car built by John Tojeiro. It was followed by the Aceca coupé in 1954 and the four-seater Greyhound in 1959.

American racing driver Caroll Shelby was interested in the Ace's competition successes and this led to the Ford V8-engined AC Cobra of which 1,070 were made between 1962 and 1969. The fastest of these, the 427-cubic inch (seven-litre) version introduced in 1965, developed 400bhp, which allowed 0-60mph acceleration in 4.2 seconds and a top speed exceeding 265km/h (165mph).

Under the guidance of Derek Hurlock, son of William, AC built the ME3000 (with a Ford three-litre V6 engine) which went into production in January 1979.

Fewer than 100 were made and, following company losses, news came in 1984 that a Scottish businessman had bought the company and formed AC (Scotland) Ltd. This company went out of business in 1985, having made just 30 Ford-engined cars at the Glasgow factory, but the AC name was kept alive by Surrey-based engineer Brian Angliss, whose Autokraft company assembles AC Cobras under licence from Ford.

In late 1986 Angliss revealed a new targa-top two-seater, the AC Ace, which employed a Ford engine and running gear and had been styled by members of Ford's European design group. One year later Ford acquired a controlling interest in AC, retaining Angliss as its managing director, and decided to substantially alter the Ace prior to its delayed launch in 1990.

Adler

Germany
1900–1939

The Adler company was well known as a manufacturer of bicycles and typewriters before it began building cars in Frankfurt am Main in 1900, initially with De Dion engines. From 1902, the company made its own engines and the arrival of Edmund

Right: The 1913 Morgan-Adler Carette seated driver and passenger in tandem

Above: Four-cylinder 12hp Adler
Right: 1910 two-seater with 12hp engine

Rumpler in 1903 led to much-improved designs. By 1905, most models had four-cylinder engines, although there were still singles and vee-twins. Success was such that, by 1914, one car in every five in Germany was an Adler.

A selection of the more popular pre-war models reappeared in 1919. The first six-cylinder Adler arrived in 1925, later being joined by a straight-eight model in 1928. But the mainstay of the 1920s range was the 1½-litre Favorit, a four-cylinder model introduced in 1925.

The company introduced the 1½-litre Trumpf in 1932, with a front-wheel-drive layout designed by Hans Gustav Röhr, and the success of this model encouraged Adler to launch a smaller one-litre version in 1934, the Trumpf Junior. The engine size of the Trumpf was twice increased (to 1.7 then 1.9-litres), and although performance would always be modest, excellent handling helped competition versions to do well. Adlers also took 22 international long-distance records.

Rear-wheel drive was not abandoned, however. The 1½-litre engine was also offered with a conventional drivetrain layout from 1932, and the larger Adlers, including an aerodynamically styled 2½-litre six-cylinder model in 1937, would always have this configuration.

Adler production stopped with the advent of war in 1939 and, although a post-war prototype was shown in 1948, no more cars were made. The company continued to make motor-cycles until 1957.

Left: 1912 Adler 7/15hp had dual ignition
and a three-speed gearbox
Right: 1936 Adler Trumpf cabriolet

Alfa Romeo

Italy
1909 to date

The Alfa Romeo story starts in France. Car manufacturer Alexandre Darracq set up a factory at Portello on the outskirts of Milan and supplied parts from Paris for single-and twin-cylinder cars.

It was not the success he had hoped for, however, and in 1909 he sold his ailing Italian outpost to the Italian group Anonina Lombardo Fabbrica Automobil – A.L.F.A for short.

Above: 1910 Alfa Romeo with 24hp engine
Below: 1912 15/20 in racing trim

In 1915 the Romeo connection was made when Nicola Romeo took over the reins. A racing enthusiast and a great engineer, he turned the make into a world-beater.

The factory's early sidevalve and overhead-valve four-cylinder engines gave way to six- and eight-cylinder designs from designers Merosi and Jano. Later followed supercharged double-overhead-camshaft models including the three-litre eight-

Above: This 20/30hp Berlina was built in 1921

Below: The 1921 P1 racer designed by Merosi, with Sivocci at the wheel

cylinder Tipo B, the Bimotore which featured two eight-cylinder engines, and a 4.5-litre V12.

Opera singer Guiseppe Campari gave Alfa its first race victory in 1920. He also won the 1924 French Grand Prix behind the wheel of Alfa's first Grand Prix car to be used in anger, the P2 designed by Vittorio Jano.

Alfa's P3 was the first *monoposto* (single-seat) G.P. racing car. It was introduced in 1932 when regulations

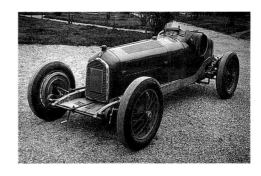

Above: 1924 supercharged P2 racer
Below: Six-cylinder RL, 1923 to 1928

Above: 1928 6C Sport Zagato 1500
Below: Finely proportioned 1932 Monza

Above: The highly successful 1932 P3

2300cc two-seat Spyder of 1932 was a direct result of racing pedigree.

We have Alfa Romeo to thank for the term GT which many would argue has been overused and abused during recent decades. The term *'gran turismo'* was applied to the supercharged six-cylinder 1750cc long-chassis sports car.

Financial complications led to the company being taken over by the Italian government in 1933. Racing was encouraged by Mussolini and at that time care of the racing team was entrusted to Enzo Ferrari.

requiring two-seater bodies were dropped. A beautiful machine of its time, it was a born winner and great drivers such as Tazio Nuvolari shared in the pleasure of steering it to victory.

Racing success always finds its way into road cars, and the exquisite straight-eight

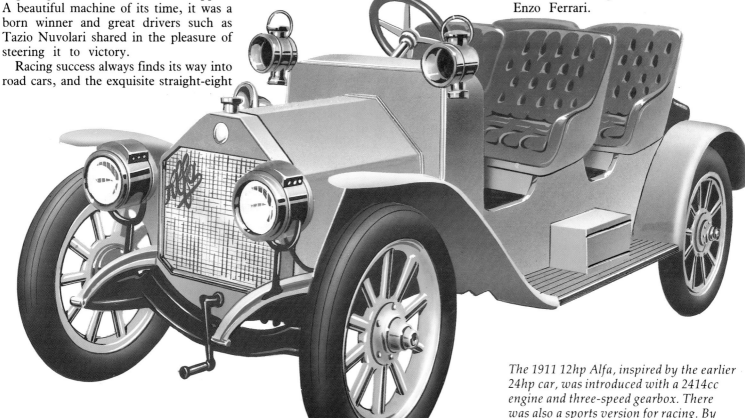

The 1911 12hp Alfa, inspired by the earlier 24hp car, was introduced with a 2414cc engine and three-speed gearbox. There was also a sports version for racing. By 1915 around 330 cars had been sold.

Above: The 6C 1750 Gran Sport of 1930 was inspired by the P2 racing car. The 1752cc six-cylinder engine featured two gear-driven overhead-camshafts and, with a Roots-type supercharger, it developed 84bhp at 4,500rpm. The body was by coachbuilder Zagato.

Below: 1936 8C 2900A

Right: 1939 6C 2500 Coloniale

The early 1930s was a glorious time for Alfa. It was building up victories which led to a total of 11 Mille Miglia and four Le Mans wins.

Many regard Alfa's greatest pre-war glory as the 1935 German Grand Prix when Nuvolari, in a 3.8-litre P3, beat the might of the Mercedes and Auto Union teams on their home territory.

Engineering genius Gioacchino Colombo worked with Ferrari in creating the Type 158 'Alfetta' which was soon back in action after World War II had ended. It dominated the 1948 Grand Prix season and, in rejuvenated form, won the first-ever world drivers' championship in 1950 driven by Giuseppe Farina.

The only other race winner that year was Juan-Manuel Fangio who also drove a Type 158 1½-litre straight-eight car with twin Roots superchargers. At the time the car was described as 'obsolete but unbeatable'.

Below: The eight-cylinder 2905cc 8C 2900 was introduced in 1937. Exquisitely styled, it was probably the fastest road car of its day; 30 were built during its two-year lifespan.

Fangio retained the F1 title for Alfa the following year. But by this time a new era had dawned. Fabulous and thrilling though the racing cars and pre-war single- and twin-cam Jano designs were with their Touring and Zagato bodywork, the world was clamoring for cheap personal transportation.

With the factory three parts destroyed during the war, Alfa Romeo had a massive task ahead. To satisfy the road market the company was back in production by 1947 when it introduced the 2.5-litre *Freccia d'Oro* (Golden Arrow) with column gear change.

In 1950 came Alfa Romeo's first four-cylinder car for 25 years, a 1900cc saloon with integral chassis-body construction. Super and Sprint versions were subsequently added followed by the *Disco Volante* (Flying Saucer) in 1952. This radical body shape by Touring of Milan

was built for publicity purposes and never went into production, though a racing version minus the startling bodywork and with a six-cylinder engine finished second in the 1953 Mille Miglia and won the Grand Prix at Merano.

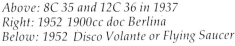

Above: 8C 35 and 12C 36 in 1937
Right: 1952 1900cc doc Berlina
Below: 1952 Disco Volante or Flying Saucer

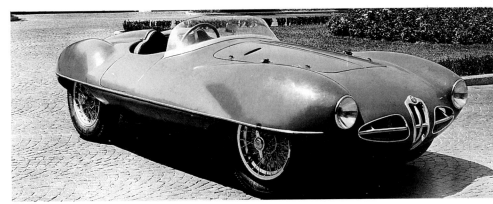

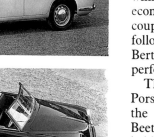

Then in 1954 Alfa Romeo introduced a car with immediate appeal for the buying public – the Giulietta. With a twin-cam four-cylinder engine of 1300cc it was a winning combination of performance and economy. It was produced in two-door coupé and four-door berlina versions followed by Pininfarina, Zagato and Bertone variants with even higher performance.

The project was overseen by former Porsche engineer Rudolf Hruschka, one of the co-ordinators on the Volkswagen Beetle. The Giulietta saloon had fallen behind schedule and when the new cars were not available to be presented as prizes for a shareholders' draw, something had to be done.

With managing director Ing. Quarino, Hruschka commissioned Bertone to prepare bodies in time for the 1954 Turin

Top left: 1953-5 1900 saloon
Centre left: 1954 six-cylinder cabriolet
Left: 1954 four-cylinder Giulietta Sprint by Bertone

show. The fastback styling of Bertone's two-door coupé proved to be a real winner. Hruschka's insistence that the car be sporting throughout had been the right recipe. The lucky shareholders found their wait worthwhile after all.

Italy experienced a tremendous growth rate in car production from 1950 to 1955 and the Giulietta was part of that success.

Above: 1300cc Giulietta Spider built around 1960

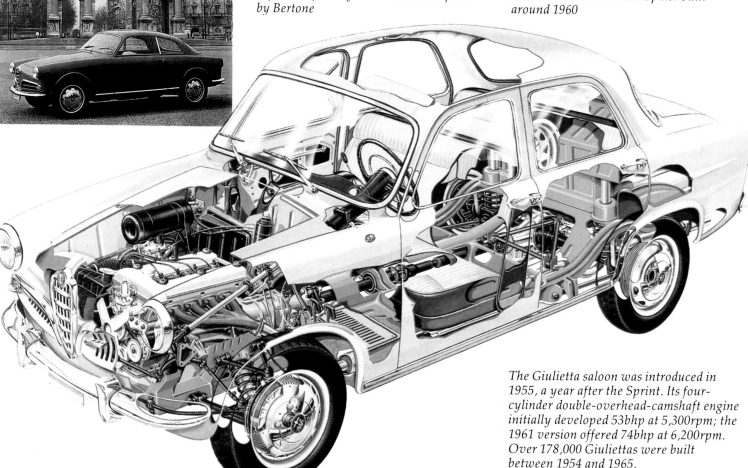

The Giulietta saloon was introduced in 1955, a year after the Sprint. Its four-cylinder double-overhead-camshaft engine initially developed 53bhp at 5,300rpm; the 1961 version offered 74bhp at 6,200rpm. Over 178,000 Giuliettas were built between 1954 and 1965.

This car and its variants became Alfa Romeo's backbone for eight years. In 1962 a 'grown up' option was offered, the larger Giulia with optional 1570cc twin-cam engine, five-speed gearbox and disc brakes.

The 1900 Super continued. Its capacity was increased to 2000cc in 1962 and a six-cylinder twin-cam 2.6-litre car introduced. All were available with a wide choice of body styles and performance specifications and they were loved for their performance and handling.

The following year construction of a new factory to replace the limited Portello works was started at Arese, also on the outskirts of Milan. From the new factory came the V8 two-litre twin-cam Tipo 33 mid-engined race car. Enlarged to three litres it won the Targa Florio, Brands Hatch 1000km race and Watkins Glen six-hour event in 1971, but the car was never without its problems, though it was instrumental in the production of a great road car in the old Alfa tradition.

This was the Bertone-styled Montreal (conceived as an exhibit for the 1967 Montreal World Fair) which used a 2.6-litre version of the twin-cam V8. A two-plus-two with fuel injection and five-speed gearbox, here was a fast road car with a pure racing engine. Top speed was quoted at 222km/h (138mph). With disc brakes all round it was based on the 1600 Giulia coupé floorpan and featured a live rear axle. While this was not regarded as

Above left: 1958-1961 2000 saloon
Above: 1971 1750 GTV
Below left: 1971 1300 Giulia Super
Below: 1971 1750 Berlina
Bottom: 1973 front-wheel-drive Alfasud

much of a plus point the car gained a glamorous reputation and was the pride of the factory, 3,925 examples being built from 1970 to 1975.

In 1968 a new Giulia with a 1779cc engine had been introduced and to boost jobs in the south of Italy the government that year persuaded Alfa Romeo to set up a manufacturing plant near Naples. It opened in 1971 with production of the 1186cc flat-four Alfasud (Alfa South). A completely new car, it featured front-wheel-drive and MacPherson-strut front suspension, belt-drive single-overhead camshafts and a four-speed transaxle.

The Hruschka design was acclaimed for its roadholding thanks to wide track and dead axle with leading and trailing arms and Panhard rod. With disc brakes all round the 63bhp car encouraged enthusiastic driving, but many found the Giugiaro styling boring.

From a marketing point of view it was a leader, however, and higher-performance versions saw that it never strayed far from pole position in the hot small-car sales war.

Also in 1971 Alfa's 1750cc road engine was bored to 1962cc and the following year the Alfetta name was revived with 1779cc four-cylinder twin-cam power and a De Dion rear axle incorporating a five-speed gearbox as used in the 1951 race car.

The 1972 Alfetta was the first production car to employ this system of front engine and rear-mounted clutch, gearbox and differential, giving excellent weight distribution.

A more economical 1.6-litre Giulia-powered version was later introduced, plus GT 1.6, 1.8 and two-litre variants.

The Alfasud became a hatchback model in 1981 and lasted until 1984 when the 33 model took over with 1350cc, 1490cc and 1712cc engines.

Top left: Bertone-styled V8-engined Montreal
Centre left: 1600 Spider with Pininfarina body
Bottom left: 1976 twin-cam Alfetta GT
Below: 1984 Alfetta Gold Cloverleaf
Opposite top: Giulietta 1.6 was introduced in 1978
Opposite centre left: 1985-specification 33 1.3 saloon
Opposite centre: High-performance GTV available with in-line four or V6 engine
Opposite centre right: The Sprint was a successful Alfasud variant
Opposite bottom: 1986 4wd 33 estate

Left: 1990-specification 75 Twin-Spark
Above: Stunning three-litre V6 164 Lusso
Below: Alfa 90 in Gold Cloverleaf trim

The Giulietta name lasted over 20 years. It was finally ousted by the 1986 '75' – so called because it was introduced to celebrate the company's 75th birthday. (This is called Milano in the United States.) Retaining the same floorpan and De Dion rear suspension the model ranges from 1779cc four-cylinder cars to 2959cc 188bhp models, all with rear-wheel-drive.

For 1988 Alfa introduced the 164 powered by a 192bhp 2959cc V6 with a 220km/h (137mph) top speed, sumptuous interior, front-wheel-drive, all-independent suspension and anti-lock braking as an option. It looks set to carry the company's national pride well into the 1990s.

Below: The Pininfarina-styled Spider was still in production in 1990, well over 20 years after its introduction in its original boat-tailed form.

Above: The 75's saloon body was also available with a three-litre V6 engine

Below: The rather strangely styled ES30 was first shown in 1989

Top: Alfa Romeo 33 1.7 Veloce
Above: 33-bodied 1.7 Sportswagon

The introduction of the 164 heralded a new start for Alfa Romeo. Whereas the eighties had seen little more than rebodied seventies cars, by the nineties Alfa was starting to be a little more adventurous with its styling and developing new, more competitive models.

The 164 was still in production in 1997 and remained almost unchanged in its 10-year production span but gained a quad cam 24-valve V6 engine in 1992.

The ES30 show car, first shown at the Geneva show in 1989, became a production model in 1990, badged as the SZ (Sport Zagato). This hard-top sports coupé with its 3-litre V6 and brutally-styled glassfibre body-work, was an instant classic. A convertible version, the RZ, became available in 1992. Unfortunately, sales were not good and the model was soon dropped from the range.

Previous page: Alfa Romeo Nuvola concept car
Top: The 145 hatchback was launched in 1994 with the old four-cylinder boxer engine but received the new twin-cam four in 1996
Right: The new Spider was launched in 1994

The first car in the range to be replaced was the quirkily-styled but outmoded 75 or Milano, in 1992. The replacement model was the 155, launched initially with 2.0-litre Twin Spark and 2.5-litre V6 engines. Alfa's new corporate identity was beginning to form with the new car carrying a similar Alfa Romeo grille that was more integrated into the front end, as first seen on the 164. The range was expanded with the addition of a 1.8-litre twin spark engine and a rapid 2.0-litre four-wheel-drive version.

The 145, launched in 1994 to replace the ageing 33 saw even more innovative design. This stylish little three-door hatchback had a distinctive step in the door window-frames and an unusual tailgate treatment with a notch in the lower edge of the rear windshield. A notchback, five-door version, the 146, followed a year later. The four-cylinder boxer engine, developed originally for the Alfasud, remained determinedly under the hood until 1996, when it was replaced by the new Fiat-based twin-cam twin-spark engine

Top: The GTV, like the Spider, was styled in conjunction with Pininfarina and gained the 3.0-litre V6 engine in 1996

Above: The 146 was a small Alfa for those who found the styling of the mechanically similar 145 too quirky for their tastes

Left: Alfa's design studio came up with the beautiful 156 for 1997

in 1.4-, 1.6-, 1.8- and 2.0-litre forms. Unusually for a marque with such a sporting history, the 145/146 range is also available with a 1.9-litre turbodiesel engine on some markets.

Alfa's greatest move in recent years was its replacement of the original Spider in 1993. By this stage, no amount of plastic add-ons or spoilers could keep the car looking up to date. The replacement Spider, not launched until 1996, is one of the most striking production cars on the road today, together with the hardtop version the GTV, both products of a collaboration between Pininfarina and the Alfa Romeo/Fiat design studio. These new cars carried a completely new engine for Alfa. Yes, it was still a twin-cam 2.0-litre design, but the new power unit, part of Fiat's new family of modular engines, used a Fiat block with an exclusive twin-cam, twin-spark cylinder head. An output of 150bhp gave reasonable performance, but the excellent suspension was capable of dealing with a whole lot more, despite the limitations of its front-wheel-drive layout. The solution was the addition of the 3.0-litre, quad-cam V6, giving the car the performance that its stunning looks deserved. A turbocharged 2.0-litre V6-engined GTV was also available on certain markets.

Allard

Great Britain
1937–1960

Sydney Allard was born in 1910 and started business in 1930 as Adlards Motors Ltd. in small premises at Putney, South London.

The name came from building firm Roberts Adlard which Sydney's father had acquired.

Allard was successful in trials with a Ford V8 fitted with a Bugatti tail. The first version was built for sale in 1937.

A total of 12 Allards were built between 1937 and September 1939, ranging from trials cars to four-seater tourers.

The Allard Motor Company Ltd. was formed in February 1945, although Adlards Motors Ltd. remained in business until 1976, and new premises were acquired in nearby Clapham.

Above: 1953-4 M2X 4-seater convertible

The new range of cars used mostly Ford components and bodies by Whittingham and Mitchel and Paramount Sheet Metal. The first production cars were ready by 1946, six leaving the factory that year.

Above: The spacious Safari estate

Models included the V8-engined K two-seaters and L four-seaters. The P-Type saloon was added to the range in time for the 1948 London Motor Show.

All Ford dealerships were listed as

The Allard J2 was introduced in 1949. With a 3197cc Mercury engine producing 140bhp, it could reach 177km/h (110mph). A limited number of J2 replicas have been built recently in Ontario, Canada.

official Allard agents and the company was represented in several countries.

Allards continued to be competitive in sporting events, using engines such as Cadillacs, Chryslers and Dodges.

Production of the larger cars fell during the late 1950s and the last three had 3.4-litre Jaguar engines. This was ironic because it was Jaguar's success with the XK120 which had been partly responsible for Allard's falling sales.

The company won a contract with the London Ambulance Service in 1959 to convert B.M.C. and Bedford chassis to De Dion axles, and other work included tuning Ford Anglias, sold as Allardettes.

Allard also became world distributors and manufacturers of Shorrock super-chargers.

Sydney Allard died in April 1966 but the business was carried on by Reg Canham, who controlled the Ford dealership of Adlards, and Sydney's son Alan, who put his efforts into superchargers, tuning and

sunroofs. Allards closed in 1976 and Alan Allard ran a factory at Daventry until 1975, moving to Ross-on-Wye and founding Allard Turbochargers.

Replica Allard J2s have been made in Ontario, Canada, but production has been extremely limited.

Below: 1952 Allard J2X

Alpine

France
1955 to date

Based at Dieppe in northern France, Automobiles Alpine produces a single-model range of rear-engined grand-touring cars with a decidedly sporting bias. The Alpine factory has always relied on an association with Renault for its components.

The first Alpine appeared in 1955, making its debut in the Mille Miglia race in the hands of its sponsor Jean Redélé whose father was the Renault agent in Dieppe during the early 1950s. Redélé rallied a modified 750cc Renault 4CV, winning a Coupe des Alpes in 1954 and the 750cc class in the Mille Miglia.

Having obtained an engineering degree, the 33-year-old Redélé gave up the car-repair side of the family business and set up in limited production using the name Société Automobiles Alpine. The first car was called the Mille Miles to celebrate his racing successes in the Mille Miglia. This vehicle was a glassfibre-bodied coupé styled by Michelotti and built in Paris by Chappe Frères, with Renault 4CV running gear which could include Redélé's own five-speed gearbox. The A106 as it was termed was a class-winner in the 1956 Mille Miglia, and although production was fairly limited, by 1957 customers could order cabriolet styling and more-powerful 845cc or bored-out 904cc and 948cc Dauphine engines.

Above: Alpine 1600 Coupé with A110 body
Below right: Le Mans, 1966, with Alpine Renault leading the pack at Tertre Rouge

Right: Delageneste and Chinisse co-drove 1.3-litre car at Le Mans in 1967
Below right: 3-litre A220 at Le Mans, 1968

Alpine evolution kept pace with the development of Renault production models, and included the steel-bodied A107 prototype and, in 1961, a 2+2 coupé and Tour de France Berlinette. The factory was producing around 100 units a year by now, and in 1963 came the classic rear-engined rear-wheel-drive A110, which remained in production for 15 years, during which time engine capacity rose in stages from 1108cc to 1800cc.

The A110 was highly successful in

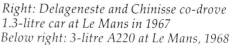

Below left: One-litre Alpine Renault at Le Mans, 1963
Below: Le Mans, 1964, Delageneste and Morrogh

Far left: 1.3-litre A210 of Nicholas and Andruet
Left: Specially prepared 1966 Le Mans car

competitions, finishing first, second and third in the 1971 Monte Carlo Rally. Alpine was by now responsible for the Renault Competitions Department, and also heavily sponsored by Elf, the French state-owned petrol company, and the A110 took the World Rally Championship in 1973.

Alongside development of the road cars, Alpines were also campaigned in the World Sportscar Championship, where cars based on the A210 regularly carried off the Index of Performance trophy at Le Mans. Real glory came in 1978 – four years after Automobiles Alpine was taken over by Renault – when the Renault-Alpine A442 drive by Jean-Pierre Jaussaud and Didier Pironi won Le Mans outright.

Forays into single-seater racing were less successful but, by 1969, the company had moved into new premises, and the new A310 was launched in 1971. Initially powered by a tuned Renault 16 engine producing 140bhp, then the 2664cc V6 engine from the Renault 30 saloon, this was sold in all Renault dealerships and covered by Renault guarantee. It was manufactured in a number of countries including Spain, Brazil and Mexico, and achieved a peak production of around 2,000 units a year.

Ten years later, its replacement, the 151mph Renault Alpine GTA V6 was introduced, and was available in normally aspirated or turbocharged form. In some quarters it is seen as a stylish and modern alternative to the Porsche 911.

Below: Launched in 1963 with an 1108cc Renault Gordini engine, the A110 took first, second and third place in the 1971 Monte Carlo Rally with a 1600cc unit.

Alvis

Great Britain
1920–1967

The Alvis 12/50 is one of the most famous of all vintage cars. Produced from 1923 until 1932, it had a 1½-litre overhead-valve four-cylinder engine, although the cubic capacity varied from model to model.

Alvis was founded in Coventry by T.G. John in 1919, and he led the company for its first quarter-century. The first car was a bought-out design, the sidevalve 10/30, but this soon evolved into a 12/40 and then into the overhead-valve 12/50, with which Alvis established itself as the builder of high-quality sporting machinery.

Finances were precarious, however, and a receiver was appointed in 1924. Yet Alvis survived to experiment with front-wheel-drive, both in supercharged 1½-litre eight-cylinder competition models, and in four-cylinder road cars which were too expensive to sell well. Rear-wheel-drive returned for the 1930s, when Alvis produced a range of well-engineered and rakishly styled six-cylinder models with evocative names like Silver Eagle, Crested Eagle, Speed Twenty, and so on. The 4.3-litre model of the late 1930s was one of only a handful of British cars which could attain 100mph (160km/h).

During World War II, Alvis concentrated on the aero-engines which it had begun to build in 1935 and on military vehicles. After 1945, these would keep the

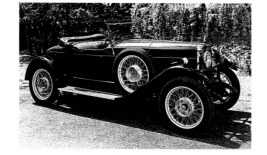

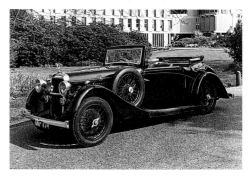

Above: 1934 Speed 20 Tourer by Cross and Ellis
Below: 1936 Silver Eagle drophead coupé

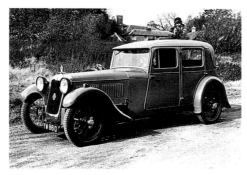

Centre: 1927 12/50 'Beetleback'
Right: 1928 front-wheel-drive 12/75

company afloat, while the cars became a secondary activity. The first post-war car was the TA14, which picked up pre-war themes, but in 1950 a new independent front suspension chassis and three-litre engine arrived in the TA21. The majority of both models had saloon or drophead bodies, although a few sports tourers were built and designated TB14 or TB21. The basic chassis design remained unchanged for the TC21/100 'Grey Lady' 160km/h (100mph) sports saloon of 1955 and the range of TD21, TE21 and TF21 models fitted with the Graber-styled two-door body after 1958. Alvis merged with Rover in 1965, but plans for new models were never realized. The last car was built in August 1967 and the company concentrated thereafter solely on military vehicles.

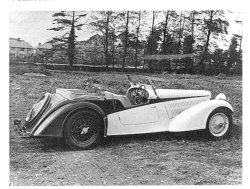

Above: 1938 Speed 25 saloon by Charlesworth
Left: 1939 short-chassis 4.3-litre by Vanden Plas
Centre left: 1946 TA14 shooting brake
Bottom left: 1953 TC21/100 Grey Lady
Right: 1955 TD21 Grey Lady
Below: The last Alvis, the TF21, was built in 1967

A.M.C.

U.S.A.
1968-1988

In 1954 Nash and Hudson merged and under the presidency of George Romney became known as American Motors Corporation. Romney concentrated company efforts on the 1950-introduced Nash Rambler, which by 1957 had expanded to a 20-model range. Around 1959 A.M.C. reintroduced the Ambassador with a 5359cc V8 engine as its top-of-the-range model, while at the same time reviving the six-cylinder Rambler as the American. The cars were well received, with production continuing until 1970, when the Rambler was dropped and A.M.C. acquired Kaiser-Jeep Corp. In 1974 production of the Ambassador ceased.

One of the most exciting cars produced by A.M.C. was the sporty and very successful four-seater Javelin introduced in 1968 with a choice of either a 'small' 3.8-litre V6 or a 3.7-, 5.6- or 6.4-litre V8 engine. Front disc brakes were optional on the V8 cars, at a time when big drum brakes were the norm.

The ANX two-seater and the hatchback Gremlin were introduced in quick succession, while in 1974 A.M.C. adopted a new approach when it announced the sporting Pacer series.

Top: 1956 Rambler station wagon
Above: The Javelin SST, introduced in 1968

In 1975 an agreement with Renault allowed A.M.C. to build and sell the Renault R18, while in the same year the Spirit was introduced to replace the Gremlin, available as a hatchback or saloon.

In the late 1980s A.M.C. was building both the Renault Encore (1397cc engine) and the Renault Alliance (1397cc or 1721cc) in addition to its own Eagle Series saloons and station wagons with either a 105bhp 2460cc engine or the 112bhp 4228cc six-cylinder unit.

In 1980 Renault purchased a 41.6 per cent holding in A.M.C., and finally Chrysler bought A.M.C. in 1987 for its Jeep line and assembly facilities, but not its name.

Top: 1964 Rambler Ambassador
Above: 1974 Pacer hatchback
Right: A.M.C.'s 1984 Jeep CJ-7 Laredo

Left: The 1974 Pacer placed great emphasis on passenger space and visibility. It was short but wide, and was claimed to have windows covering a third of its exterior. Straight-six engines of 3802 and 4228cc were offered, with manual or automatic transmission.

Amilcar

France
1921–1939

The famous French firm of Amilcar was established in 1921, producing sports models which could be enjoyed to the full in that country at the time. The firm's founders were Messieurs Lamy and Akar, whose names were blended to form the company title.

The company's first cars – the CC, CS and 4C Types, designed by Edmond Moyet – were sporting two-seaters which used one-litre, sidevalve four-cylinder power units. In 1924 the nine-horsepower, overhead-valve CGS was introduced with a top speed approaching 128km/h (80mph) and braking on the front wheels as well as the rears. The lower CGSS model (which was more powerful still) became available two years later. This car – the Surbaissé model, with its 1100cc power unit and abbreviated motorcycle-type mudguards – is very much sought after today. The models to date featured simple chassis design and narrow, streamlined bodywork.

Amilcar built cars with specifications and performance which sound creditable today, let alone in the 1920s. The C6 Course, for example, also introduced in 1926, featured a twin-overhead-camshaft six-cylinder engine which propelled the car to 193km/h (120mph). This car was very successful in racing.

Another Amilcar which gained recognition for its handling and performance was the overhead-camshaft straight-eight C8 of

Above: 1925 Amilcar CGS Grand Sport

1928, which gave 128km/h (80mph) from 1800cc.

The company's advanced, sporting products provided exhilarating motoring and in the firm's heyday during the late 1920s cars were being built at the rate of some 12,000 per year.

For the 1930s Amilcar offered a two-litre version of the C8; an M-Type (initially with 1250cc, later 1700cc); a five-horsepower Type C (from 1933); a 12-horsepower N7 (powered by Delahaye) and a 14-horsepower G36 model.

Just prior to World War II Hotchkiss produced some fascinating 1200cc Amilcar saloons with lightweight unitary-construction bodywork, all-round independent suspension and front-wheel-drive.

Sadly, there were to be no post-war Amilcars.

Below: 1927 CGSS Surbaissé model
Bottom: 1928 ohc straight-eight C8

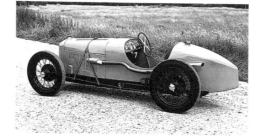

Above: Early Amilcars were CC, CS and 4C models
Right: 1926 C6 production racer
Below: The CGSS Surbaissé was a further developed version of the CGS, and was both lower and faster than its predecessor. Later models featured a differential.

Armstrong–Siddeley
Great Britain
1919–1960

The Coventry-based Siddeley-Deasy company merged with the car-making side of Armstrong-Whitworth to form Armstrong-Siddeley in 1919, and the first fruit of the merger was that year's 30hp model, a large and solidly built six-cylinder machine which lasted until 1932. This was joined in 1921 by a scaled-down 18hp model, which gained an enlarged engine in 1925 and was redesignated a 20hp two years later.

Above: 1926 14hp with a 1825cc engine

The six-cylinder models were joined by a four-cylinder 14hp in 1925, but this lasted only until 1929, when the company reverted to its all-six-cylinder policy. In that year, too, appeared the first models with a Wilson preselector gearbox, which was standardized across the range in 1933. The most popular pre-war model was the 12hp, however, introduced in 1928 and offered with a wide variety of body styles. Its sidevalve engine was the smallest six-cylinder unit available on the British market but, after 1936, all models had six-cylinder engines.

Above: 1934 12hp tourer, a popular model
Below: 1930 30hp six-cylinder landaulette

The 1991cc overhead-valve engine first seen in 1938 also powered the 1946 16hp model, available in saloon and drophead styles with names evocative of the warplanes built by the related aircraft company. The range was revised in 1948 and centred on an 18hp engine, but new and distinctive styling arrived in 1953 on the Sapphire 346 luxury saloon. From 1958, the more powerful Star Sapphire was offered, but even a proper automatic transmission and disc front brakes could not disguise the fact that the separate-chassis design of these cars was behind the times. Sales of the smaller Sapphire 234 and 236 saloons, introduced

Above: The rather formal 1936 20/25
Left: 1928 30hp six-cylinder London

Above: 1935 20hp four-light saloon
Below: 1936 20/25 touring saloon

in 1955 with bodies partly panelled in Hiduminium aircraft alloy, proved disappointing and these were withdrawn in 1958. Production ceased in 1960 when the parent Hawker-Siddeley concern merged with the Bristol aircraft company.

Above: 1953 Sapphire four-light saloon
Below: 1956 Sapphire 346 automatic

Arrol-Johnston/ Arrol-Aster

Scotland 1895–1929

It was not until the mid-1880s that the first reliable petrol-driven cars appeared, developed independently in Germany by Gottlieb Daimler and Karl Benz. Meanwhile in Scotland, locomotive engineer George Johnston, disenchanted with his experimental steam tram, turned his hand to the internal-combustion engine, developing a four-piston, opposed-twin engine with combustion occurring between two pistons moving in opposite directions, but connected by rocking beams to the same single crank-shaft.

This engine was mounted in a heavy dog-cart and launched in 1895 by the company then managed by engineer Sir William Arrol, of Forth Bridge fame, with production continuing until 1906.

In 1905 a 3023cc 12/15hp car using the same opposed-piston engine was unveiled, while in the same year a 3795cc opposed-twin Arrol-Johnston beat the Rolls-Royce of Percy Northey to win the very first Isle of Man Tourist Trophy Race. More orthodox engines were then developed in the form of the 1906 24/30hp vertical four of 4654cc and the 1907 8832cc unit, with the old horizontal-twin 12/15 model being phased out in 1909.

In the same year T.C. Pullinger, previously of Darracq and Humber, joined the company and produced a new range of cars with a 15.9hp 2835cc engine, a dashboard radiator and four-wheel braking, making Arrol-Johnston and Crossley the first British manufacturers to introduce this controversial braking system. With the foot pedal operating the front wheels and the hand-brake the rear ones, an inexperienced driver could quite easily lose control and spin the car.

Model followed model until in 1913 production moved from Paisley to Dumfries, where some 50 electric cars were built for Edison, while some six years laer, the 'unsellable and unreliable' 2651cc

Above: Arrol-Johnston c. 1901

Below: Charlesworth-bodied 15.9hp model

Victory model was announced. Around 1925 a 3290cc Empire model was built for the Colonies and in 1927 Arrol-Johnston merged with Aster – makers of the sleeve-valve engine. The company's final model, the straight-eight sleeve-valve 70hp 3292cc Arrol-Aster, was unsuccessful, and the company closed down in 1929.

Below: 1927 six-cylinder model

Aston Martin

Great Britain 1922 to date

Aston Martin was registered as a company in 1913. It was formed by engineer Robert Bamford and wealthy car enthusiast Lionel Martin, and based at Kensington, London.

The company's first car was a one-off competition machine using a 1400cc four-cylinder Coventry-Simplex engine grafted into a 1908 Grand Prix des Voiturettes Isotta-Fraschini chassis.

The name of the car – Aston Martin – was evolved from Martin's successful outings at the Aston Clinton hill-climb in Buckinghamshire in his 10hp Singer.

World War I cut short the company's car development and Bamford resigned in 1920 with Martin's wife taking over his share. Several racing cars were built – such as a double-overhead-camshaft car ordered by Count Louis Zborowski – but it was to be three years before the first road-going cars were offered to the public.

But despite racing successes, the company reaped no profits and went into receivership in November 1924.

The firm was bought by Birmingham-based consulting engineers Renwick and Bertelli.

The new Aston Martin announced for the 1927 Olympia Show used the four-cylinder overhead-cam 10hp engine Bertelli had designed for the Enfield Allday (one car was built before the acquisition of Aston Martin).

Production moved to a new factory at Feltham, Middlesex, but Renwick withdrew support. Bertelli managed to gain the backing of various people including P. C. Kidner of Vauxhall.

Production of the first series of cars totalled just 19, with a mixture of saloons, tourers and two competition two-seaters. The racers, built by Bertelli's brother, won the Rudge Whitworth Cup in the 1928 Le Mans race.

By 1931 the company was in trouble yet again, mainly because of the high costs of

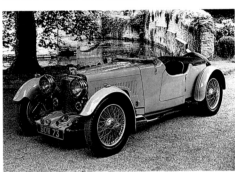

Above: 1927 T-type tourer
Below: 1933 2/4 Le Mans

The first Aston Martin, made available to the public in 1923. It had a 1.5-litre Coventry Simplex engine with a Rubery Owen chassis and, unusual for those days, front-wheel brakes.

the racing programme. It changed hands twice, ending up in the hands of London motor distributor Lance Prideaux-Brune and R. Gordon Sutherland, son of a wealthy ship-owner.

Bertelli's skills and Sutherland's money combined to produce a flourishing company, and the 1930s saw many racing successes, including the Le Mans Tourist Trophy.

Only the 1½-litre engine designed by Bertelli in 1926 was offered. It was replaced by a two-litre overhead-cam unit in 1936, designed by Bertelli and Claude Hill, and about 140 saloons and two-seaters were made up to the start of World War II.

The last pre-war model was the Atom which had independent front suspension and – in the end – a new pushrod engine.

Above: The DB3 sports racer

Above: DB3, developed into 1955 DB3S

Above: Two-litre, built from 1936 to 1939

Control of Aston Martin was taken over by tractor manufacturer David Brown in February 1947, and the DB1 went into production the following year, using the pushrod engine developed just before the outbreak of war.

David Brown then bought Lagonda and used that company's 2½-litre double-overhead-camshaft in-line six, designed by W. O. Bentley, for the DB2. That went into production in May 1950, followed by the DB3. All production was transferred to Newport Pagnell, Buckinghamshire, in 1955.

Below: 1950 DB2 with 2.6-litre engine

The 1959 DB4 was the start of a new breed because it did not use the old Atom's chassis and Lagonda engine. It was a two-door fastback coupé or convertible, with the Lagonda Rapide offered to customers who wanted a four-door body.

The 3.7-litre DB4 gave way to the four-litre DB5, DB6 and DBS. The DBS gained a 5.3-litre V8 in September 1969.

The losses involved in this development, however, were so great that Aston Martin was sold to Company Developments Ltd. in February 1972. The workforce was cut and all six-cylinder cars dropped.

But by December 1974, the company was insolvent. Much of its money had been spent adapting the V8 for the American market. Canadian Rolls-Royce distributor George Minden and American Peter Sprague formed a new company – Aston Martin Lagonda (1975) Ltd. Additional cash came from sources including Sheffield Steel.

The company had changed hands again by 1981, being bought by the chairman of Pace Petroleum, Victor Gauntlett, and Tim Healey, chairman of CH Industrials.

Above: 1960 DB4 GT capable of 244km/h (152mph)
Below: 1964 DB5 was a fast tourer
Bottom: Early DBS with straight-six engine

Above: Six-cylinder DBS

Above: 1968 Aston Martin DB6

Above: 1968 DB6 Volante convertible

Aston Martin Tickford was established, producing luxury versions of production cars from other manufacturers.

Production in the early 1980s concentrated on the Aston Martin Vantage saloon and Volante convertible and the William Towns-designed Lagonda saloon. Production was running at four cars a week by the autumn of 1985 by which time Gauntlett owned 25 per cent of the marque and the Greek Livanos shipping family the remainder.

Ford acquired control of the company in September 1987 and the new Aston Martin Virage was announced at the end of 1988, replacing the familiar V8 cars. An open-top version of the Virage, called Volante, followed a year later.

Below: 1987 Aston Martin Vantage Zagato, built in extremely limited numbers

Above: V8-powered Volante convertible

Above: Aston Martin Lagonda

Above: V8-powered Virage, announced at the 1988 Motor Show

Below: The dramatically angular Aston Martin Lagonda was a triumph of engineering and technical innovation, but has often been criticized for its looks. The 5.3-litre V8 engine gives it a top speed of 225km/h (140mph).

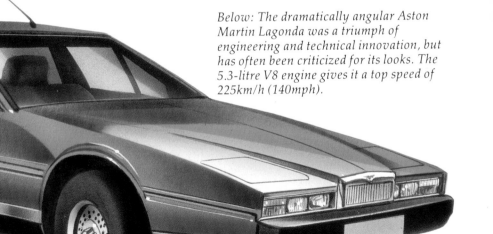

The Aston Martin range, consisting only of Virage and Volante, continued unchanged until 1992 when the new Vantage model was launched at the Birmingham Motor Show. This extremely high performance version of the Virage sported flared wheel arches, deeper chin spoiler and had an altogether more aggressive look. Under the hood lay one of the most powerful production car engines of the time. By fitting twin Roots-type Eaton superchargers, Aston Martin engineers managed to raise the power output of the hand-built alloy V8 to over 550bhp. A six-speed gearbox was also added to make better use of the extra power. Speeds of nearly 180mph (290km/h) were attainable in this luxury heavyweight and the mighty engine could take its super-rich owners to 60mph (100km/h) in a shade over 4.5 seconds.

In 1996 the standard Virage was updated with prettier, softer lines and an increase in power from 330 to 350bhp.

The biggest news at Aston Martin during the 1990s was the new DB7, launched in 1993. Available in fixed-head coupé or open-top Volante forms (from 1996), the handsome DB7 was a very welcome new model to the range. With a straight six engine, designed by TWR, the supercharged DB7 was the real spiritual successor to the long-dead DB6.

Above: The Virage was renamed the V8 in 1996

Above: 1997 DB7 Volante

Above: 1997 V8 Volante

Above: The fearsome 550bhp V8 Vantage

Above: The DB7 coupé was the 'cheap' Aston   *Below: Lagonda concept car by Vignale*

Asia Motors

Asia Motors, owned by Korean manufacturer Kia, is one of the many companies worldwide building a vehicle that is very obviously influenced by the original wartime Jeep. In fact it was used by the Korean Army, in more basic trim, long before the western world was offered it as a recreational fun vehicle. The Asia Rocsta, launched in 1994, was available with a 1.8-litre gasoline or 2.2-litre diesel engine. There were two body styles, a hardtop and a convertible. The Jeep styling was modernized with the use of plenty of black plastic, some graphics, and a set of alloy wheels. As is typical of this kind of vehicle, the performance figures could be measured with an hour-glass rather than a stop-watch, especially for the diesel model.

Above: The Rocsta's low price and rugged build meant it made a good heavy-duty working vehicle for farmers

Left: Asia Motors really tried to push the Rocsta as a lifestyle vehicle, but it didn't have the fashionable image of the Japanese four-wheel-drive recreational vehicles

Below: The car's soft top was a crude affair, as on most Jeep-type vehicles, but it was more popular than the hard-top model

Auburn

U.S.A.
1900–1937

The first Auburn was built in 1900 by Frank and Morris Eckhardt, who sold small numbers of their early models in and around Auburn, Indiana, and named their company after that town. Their first proper production model was a single-cylinder runabout with chain drive, introduced in 1903, but further models were gradually added to the range, and the twin-cylinder engines introduced in 1905 continued until a four-cylinder model with a bought-in engine arrived in 1910. A six-cylinder engine was added to the range in 1912.

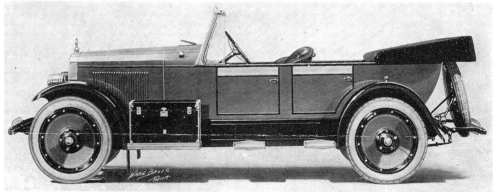

Above: 1904 Auburn runabout

Four- and six-cylinder models were offered through to 1919, and it was possible to order right-hand or left-hand steering after 1914. Engines were still bought in, from Continental, Rutenber, and Teetor. The Eckhardts sold out to a group of Chicago businessmen in 1919, and that year's Beauty Six model betrayed more conscious styling. It evolved two years later into the 6-51 sports model, but production figures remained modest. The 1923 Auburns had either Continental or Weidely six-cylinder engines, but that year was a bad one for the U.S. motor industry and by 1924 Auburn was in trouble.

That year, however, the company was bought out by Errett Lobban Cord. Cord appointed James Crawford as Chief

Engineer and had the entire range redesigned for 1925. The engineering of the new models was so advanced that almost no changes were made before 1930. All were attractively styled and well constructed, and the Auburn name in the late 1920s came to stand for cars with handsome bodies and good performance. Four-, six- and eight-cylinder models were offered; but the four-cylinder model was dropped in 1927, as the company moved upmarket.

Although a radically-styled Cabin Speedster on the eight-cylinder 115 chassis fell victim to the Depression and was withdrawn, Auburn was remarkably unaffected by the sales slump. The year 1931 was a record one for sales, aided by new and sleek styling on the 8-98 model. Later, the company followed the trend towards multi-cylinder engines with the introduction of a 6.4-litre V12 engine in 1932, which made the Auburn the first twelve-cylinder car to sell for under $1000. But this was a bad time to be breaking into

Top: Beauty Six was announced in 1919
Above: 1925 Auburn 8-88 Sedan
Below: 1935 6-120 Sedan
Bottom: 80-8 with straight-eight engine

the luxury car market, and the V12 had to be dropped in 1934.

The 1931 designs were replaced in 1934, and a six-cylinder engine was added to the range. But it was 1935 which represented Auburn's classic year, with the addition to the 653 six-cylinder and 851 eight-cylinder ranges of a supercharged 851 model and a strikingly attractive boat-tailed Speedster body, developed by Gordon Buehrig from an earlier design by Count Alexis de Saknoffsky. The addition of a Schwitzer-Cummins supercharger to the 279-cubic inch Lycoming straight-eight engine gave 150bhp, and all the supercharged Auburns were guaranteed to have been test-driven at more than 100mph (160km/h). Sadly, the company lost money on every one of these fine cars, and the range continued for only two more years; although new models were planned for 1937, none was produced and the company went into liquidation that year.

The classic speedsters have inspired several replica vehicles in more recent years, all using modern power units and chassis engineering under the 1930s-styled bodies.

Above: 1935 851 available with or without supercharger

The glamorous 851 Speedster was guaranteed capable of 161km/h (100mph). The boat-tailed speedster body was adapted from an earlier design by Count Alexis de Saknoffsky.

Audi

Germany 1910–1939, 1965 to date

When August Horch left the company bearing his name to start up on his own for a second time, he was prevented from using his own name again, so he chose instead to identify the new company by the Latin word for the literal meaning in German of his own name, *horchen*; 'to listen'. The first car to be produced by Horch as an Audi, the Type B, appeared in 1910 and brought immediate success.

Reviving his connections with motor sport, Horch entered the 1911 Austrian Alpine Trials in a Type B, leading a team of drivers which included two of his engineers, Lange and Graumuller. Horch completed the event without a penalty point, entering in the same type of car the following year, then again in 1913 in a

Above: The Type E 22/50PS

Above: Dr Horch with his 14/38PS

Above: The 1929-32 Zwickau had a Rickenbacker-designed engine
Far left: Eight-cylinder Type R also known as Imperator
Bottom: The Type K, powered by a 3.5-litre overhead-valve engine producing 50bhp, finally succeeded the Type C

Type C. The Type C won that year and the year after, to become known as the *Alpensieger* – 'Alpine Victor'.

Other pre-war models were the Types D and E, although these were made in limited numbers. With the outbreak of hostility in 1914 Audi began producing two-ton trucks on reinforced Type C chassis, as well as military vehicles. The Types C, D and E were continued after World War I, alongside the new Type G, although Horch's own personal interest in the company had waned with the inevitable creative stagnation during the war and he left Audi in 1920.

By 1922 the long-running Type C was superseded by the Type G, and two years later Audi began building its range of six- and eight-cylinder cars. The unsuccessful Type R Imperator of 1928 is considered to be the last of the true Audis, since after

that time the company became increasingly involved in assembling other manufacturers' components.

It was also in 1928 that J. S. Rasmussen of D.K.W. took the major shareholding in

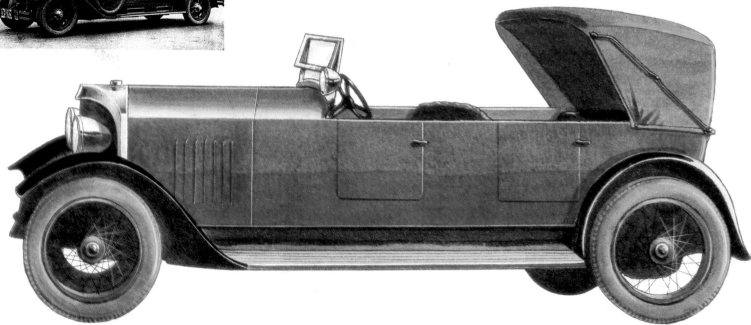

Below: The Type 225 in roadster form

Below: Audi Front sport cabriolet

Above: 1934 fwd Type 225 Front

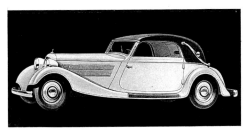

the company. He brought with him the design and manufacturing rights to the Rickenbacker engine from the U.S.A. German-built engines of this type were used in subsequent Audi models.

In 1931 a smaller Audi with a D.K.W. chassis and an 1100cc Peugeot engine was produced, and the year after that Audi, along with D.K.W., Wanderer, and Horch, became part of Auto-Union. Two Wanderer-powered front-wheel-drive models followed, and sold well in the years leading up to World War II, although the last pre-war model was the rear-driven Type 920.

Far left: 3.2-litre saloon built in 1938
Left: 1939-40 Audi A6

After the war Audi was nationalized, together with the other Auto-Union companies, as part of Industrie-Vereinigung Volkseigner Fahrzeugwerke, and the Audi factory at Zwickau was used to build D.K.W.-based cars. This only lasted until 1949 when Auto-Union re-established itself with a Mercedes-Benz majority shareholding.

The Audi name was allowed to lapse until after 1965, when Volkswagen gained a majority shareholding and a new front-wheel-drive saloon was introduced. By the end of 1968 sales had picked up and the Audi range had been considerably extended.

In 1969 Audi merged with N.S.U. to form Audi N.S.U. Auto-Union AG, although N.S.U. production ceased eight years later. Under V.W. control, however, Audi continued to improve and develop its range, with May 1973 seeing the one millionth Audi car sold.

Among the company's technological milestones have been the five-cylinder engine, first launched in the 100 Series during the late 1970s, turbocharging and four-wheel drive, the latter with the Quattro introduced in 1980/81.

Above: Auto Union Monza Coupé
Below: Auto Union 1700 saloon

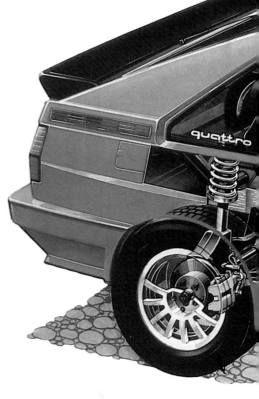

Above: The short-wheelbase Quattro Sport was announced at the 1983 Frankfurt Motor Show with a five-cylinder double-overhead-camshaft engine and an innovative four-wheel-drive transmission. Quattros took first and second places in the 1983 R.A.C. rally.

Above left: The 1972 four-cylinder Audi 80
Above: The 1977 100 saloon, the first Audi with a five-cylinder engine

The Audi Quattro and short-wheelbase Quattro Sport, both combining high performance with supercar standards of roadholding, won practically every major competition for which they were entered, leading both Audi and its Volkswagen parent to introduce four-wheel-drive on an increasing number of their road-going models. The four rings of the Audi badge, incidentally, represent the four companies originally absorbed into the Auto-Union.

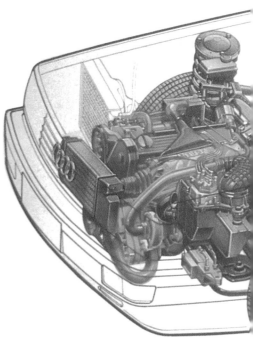

Above: 20-valve Quattro Coupé provides 220bhp

Above: Five-cylinder 100 Avant 2.3E

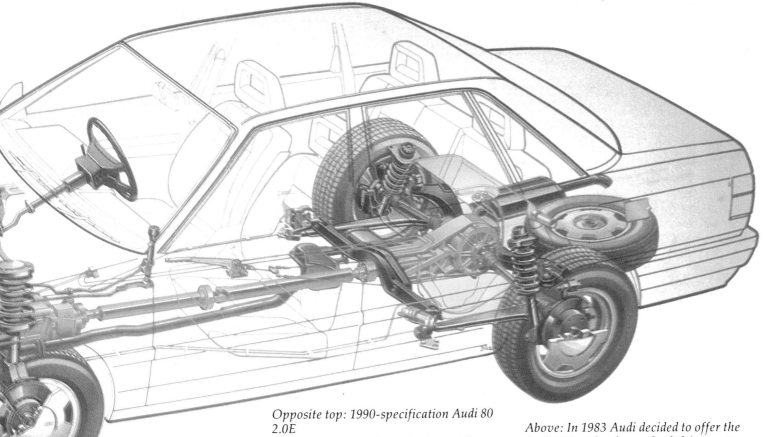

Opposite top: 1990-specification Audi 80 2.0E
Opposite centre: The turbocharged five-cylinder 100 saloon
Opposite bottom: 170bhp Coupé Quattro 20V

Above: In 1983 Audi decided to offer the Audi 200 with a four-wheel-drive system derived from the company's Quattro rally cars. In this form the 200 enjoys excellent traction and very good handling.

Audi's rapid improvement during the 1980s continued with a vengeance into the next decade. The 80 and 90 range of 1986 continued unchanged until 1991 when they received a face-lift. The 90 tag, previously used to denote the use of a five-cylinder engine, was dropped and all cars were badged as 80s with models being indicated simply by their engine size. Four- and five-cylinder models remained largely unchanged but the new updated car was available with a 2.8-litre V6 giving 174bhp. The four-wheel-drive Quattro models were continued and were available with both the V6 and the 137bhp 2.0-litre 16-valve engine.

The replacement of the famous turbo-charged Quattro and its lesser (non-turbocharged) brother, the Coupé, was

Left: The Audi A6, launched in 1997, was good enough to frighten BMW. It competed directly with the BMW 5-series, which had also been updated in the same year

Right: Top of Audi's range was the A8. It used a 4.2-litre V8 in an all-aluminium bodyshell

Middle right: Audi's estate cars were always well regarded. This is a 1997 A4 estate

Bottom right: The A3 gave Audi a new entry-level car to attract a new breed of younger potential Audi buyers

Below: The 1997 Audi Cabriolet range. There was a 2.0-litre four and two V6s, one at 2.6 litres, the other at 2.8 litres

launched in 1988. The handsome new Coupé was based on 80/90 running gear and used the same four- and five-cylinder engines. The most potent model was the 230bhp S2 Quattro, but it lacked its predecessor's brutal appeal. The Coupé was dropped in 1995.

The revolutionary Audi 100 of 1983, famous for its low Cd of 0.30, was also updated in 1991. It gained the V6 engine and more aggressive styling. The similarly-bodied 200 was dropped in favour of a new model, the V8, sharing the 100's new bodyshell. A blatant attempt to rival the range-topping models of BMW and Lexus, the Audi lacked the sporting character of the former and the refinement of the latter.

The company's next attempt at a large executive express was a great deal more successful. Launched in early 1994, the new alloy-bodied car was initially available in front-wheel-drive 2.8 V6 or 4.2-litre engine Quattro forms. A 3.7-litre V8 arrived in 1995 and a new 30-valve 2.8-litre V6 the following year. Top of the range in 1997 was the 340bhp S8 with standard four-wheel-drive. The high-tech A8 had the presence and ability to rival the world's finest prestige vehicles.

Audi launched its first cabriolet in 1991. Also based on the 80/90 range, the Cabriolet was available with four- or six-cylinder engines. Appeal and sales were enhanced by the fact that Princess Diana drove one.

Audi's range underwent another great change late in 1994 with the launch of the

Above: The Audi Cabriolet, launched at the 1991 Geneva Motor Show, rose to fame as the car chosen by Princess Diana in preference to a Mercedes convertible. It was launched only with the four-cylinder engine

Right and top right: The sharply-styled A4, launched in 1994, was the successor to the old 80. It was a best-seller for Audi in the mid-1990s and was widely praised by the motoring press

Below: The A3 was a fashionable hatchback and used the next-generation Volkswagen Golf platform. The 1.8-litre four-cylinder engine had five valves per cylinder and gave 125bhp. The turbodiesel gave a healthy 90bhp

A4 and A6, to replace the 80 and 100 models. These sharply-styled new cars offered top-notch levels of ride and refinement, first-rate build quality, and were a huge improvement on their predecessors.

To complete the range, Audi added the hatchback A3, based on the floorpan of the fourth generation VW Golf and with styling that closely related it to the rest of the range.

The A6 was updated in 1997 with new sharper styling, improved ride and roadholding and better performance. This was a car to worry even Mercedes and BMW.

By the late 1990s, Audi's image was right up with BMW and the company's cars were considered as stylish alternatives to the other German luxury brands.

Austin

Great Britain
1905-1989

As a young man Herbert Austin (later Lord Austin) emigrated to Australia, where he met Frederick Wolseley, and joined the Wolseley Sheep Shearing Company. On returning to the U.K. he built his first car – a three-wheeler – for Wolseley. He also built other Wolseleys but the first Austin emerged in 1905, from Longbridge, Birmingham, home of Austins thereafter. It was a chain-driven,

four-speed 25/30hp vehicle, with a four-cylinder engine featuring detachable valve covers to allow easy access to the valves.

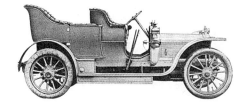

Above: 1905 25/30hp Endcliffe Phaeton

This very first car proved itself in reliability events, including the 1906 Scottish Trial.

Austin produced single-, four- and

six-cylinder cars in the early years, the biggest of which was a 9.7-litre 60hp model. The most popular of these Austins was the Twenty, with a Ten being introduced in 1910. Austin also built Gladiators for the home market, and a 1600cc ten-horsepower model, initially for export only.

By 1914, the largest 30hp Austin featured an electrically operated starter and electric lights.

Above: 1914 Vitesse Phaeton
Below: 1920 four-cylinder 20hp tourer

The Austin Seven was built from 1922 to 1939 and became one of the best-loved of all British cars. Its four-cylinder 750cc sidevalve engine gave a cruising speed of

72–80km/h (45-50mph). The car would hold four adults in reasonable comfort and was easy to drive, earning a reputation for reliability and longevity.

After World War I, Austin built just the four-cylinder Twenty, with a 3.6-litre sidevalve engine. This model was produced until 1929. Another long-lived model, the 1.7-litre Twelve, joined the Twenty in 1921, and was built until 1936, although with an enlarged (1.9-litre) engine from 1927.

A six-cylinder, 3.4-litre Twenty model was introduced in 1927, and a smaller, 2.3-litre Sixteen in 1928.

The most famous pre-World War II car of all, the Austin Seven, was introduced in 1922, with all but the earliest examples having a 747cc sidevalve four-cylinder engine developing 13bhp.

Above: The prototype Austin Seven
Below: Austin 20 tourer, c. 1927

The tough and reliable Seven was built in many versions, including tourers and saloons, and was built under licence in other countries, including France, Germany, the U.S.A. and Japan. The last 750cc Austin Seven was the Ruby, first introduced in 1934, and built until 1938, by which time Austin had introduced a larger Seven – the longer-wheelbase 900cc 'Big Seven'. However, the Ruby's engine was built under licence by Reliant until 1962.

Another Austin to find favour among many families was the famous Ten. First introduced in 1932, the model was steadily developed throughout the 1930s. The 1937 model was known as the Cambridge, and by 1939 the Ten had bodywork of semi-integral construction, as had the smaller (900cc) Eight. Power for the Ten was from an 1125cc engine developing 32bhp (later models), and giving a top speed of around 65mph (104km/h).

Austin built similarly-styled Twelves, Fourteens, Sixteens, Eighteens and Twenty-Eights until the late 1930s.

Below: Popular 14hp Ascot cabriolet, 1938

Above: Austin 10 saloon, launched in 1932
Below: 10hp Sherbourne Saloon, 1936

After World War II, Austin re-introduced the Eight, Ten and Twelve, as well as a similar-looking Sixteen, which used 1940 Austin Twelve chassis/bodywork, but which featured an overhead-valve 2.2-litre engine. The engine remained in use until the late 1960s in the four-wheel-drive Austin Gipsy, and also in Austin Taxis.

In 1947 a new luxury mode, the four-litre A125 Sheerline, was introduced, the first Austin with independent front suspension. A larger derivative was the A135 Princess, with triple carburettors.

Above: A90 Atlantic c. 1947
Above right: 1951 A40 Devon

The first all-new post-war family Austin was the 1200cc A40 Devon/Dorset (two or four doors respectively) introduced in late 1947. The A40 helped Britain's export drive of the late 1940s. The car was followed a year later by the A70 Hampshire, powered by the Austin Sixteen's engine. All the new Austins of this era were to be designated by their approximate brake horsepower output, rather than by the previously used R.A.C. rating method.

In 1949 the 2.6-litre, four-cylinder A90 Atlantic coupé was introduced, aimed at the American market. In 1951 the A70 was rebodied and named the Hereford, and a Jensen-built aluminium-bodied sports version of the A40 was introduced. The next year, the A40 Somerset, with similar styling to the Hereford, replaced the Devon and Dorset.

The 1952 model year saw the creation of the British Motor Corporation, following the merger of Austin and Morris, and the introduction of an important new Austin Seven – the A30. It had unitary-construction bodywork, with styling similar to that of the larger Austins, and a scaled-down (800cc) version of the A40's

1200cc engine. Unusual for so small a car, it was initially available only in four-door form.

In 1954 a new A40 (Cambridge) was announced, together with a larger-engined, 1489cc A50, which used identical bodywork. The A90 was a larger version, powered by a 2.6-litre six-cylinder engine.

Developments of these models were the A55 and A95/A105 saloons, from 1956 on. In that year the A35 was announced with a stronger 948cc engine and a more precise remote gearchange among other improvements.

The Metropolitan, originally produced for the American market in 1.2-litre form, was sold in the U.K. with the A50's engine and a three-speed gearbox, from 1957.

In 1958 the rubber-suspension Gipsy was introduced, along with the Farina-styled A40, which used A35 running gear. A 'hatchback' Countryman (estate-car) version was also available.

The A55, in Mark II form, was also styled by Farina from 1959, as was the A99 Westminster, now with a three-litre engine.

The most notable introduction of 1959 was, of course, the revolutinary Mini. Designed by Alec Issigonis (later Sir Alec), it provided four seats and reasonable comfort yet also had a miserly thirst for fuel.

Available under both Austin (Seven)

Above: The well-appointed A125 Sheerline
Below: A110 Westminster superseded A99

and Morris (Mini Minor) designations, the Mini featured a transversely mounted engine, sitting on top of the gearbox/differential unit, and driving tiny (ten-inch) front wheels. Underneath the box-like body the suspension was by rubber cones and the distinctive 'wheel-at-each-corner' design afforded excellent roadholding.

For use in the Mini, B.M.C.'s A Series

Above: 1964 Mini-Cooper 1275S

Above: 1300cc version of AD016

Above: 1982 Austin Mini Metro City

engine was derated to 848cc and 34bhp, although the car's light weight meant it was still capable of around 116km/h (72mph), and would reach 60mph from standstill in just over 20 seconds.

In 1960, the Mini van was introduced, as were the estate-car versions – the Traveller (Morris) and Countryman (Austin), which initially featured wooden exterior bodywork trims.

Vanden Plas Princess versions of Austins were always built to a high specification, and the three-litre model of 1960 was no exception. From 1964 a four-litre Rolls-Royce-engined Princess was available.

For 1961, the handy pickup version of the Mini was introduced, as was the first Mini-Cooper. In 997cc form, it produced 55bhp and was capable of 145km/h (90mph). Coopers later used engines of 998cc, 1071cc (making 68bhp in the Cooper S), and 1275cc (making 76bhp in the 1275S). The latter had a top speed of 160km/h (100mph), and would accelerate from rest to 96km/h (60mph) in just over 11 seconds.

Extremely successful in competition, the 1275S gained famous victories in the Monte Carlo Rallies of 1964, 1965, and 1966. And a short-stroke version of this car, the 64bhp 970S, was used with success in the under-1000cc classes of motor sport.

The Wolseley Hornet and Riley Elf were announced for the 1962 model year, these being badge-engineered luxury versions of the Mini. Also for 1962, the A55 was developed into the 1622cc A60, and the

Introduced in 1980, the Austin Mini Metro used much of the original Mini's engine, drivetrain and suspension, but carried in an entirely new body shell. The car initially had A-series engines of one-litre or 1.3-litre capacity, but by 1990 the 16-valve K-series unit was available.

A110 Westminster was introduced. Late in 1962 the A40 received the 48bhp 1098cc version of the A-Series engine.

In 1964 the Austin version of BMC's front-wheel-drive 1100 saloon was introduced, and subsequent developments of it followed those of the similar Morris models. Another front-wheel-drive Austin – the large and comfortable 1800 – arrived for 1965.

The Austin 3-litre was announced in October 1967. It was a luxurious car with body styling similar to that of the 1800, but with a 2.9-litre six-cylinder engine driving the rear wheels.

The A60 was discontinued in early 1969, and a new front-wheel-drive model arrived in April 1969 – the versatile five-door Maxi hatchback, powered by a new B-Series overhead-camshaft four-cylinder engine of 1485cc, driving through a five-speed gearbox. A 1750cc engine was available from September 1970.

In September 1969 an uprated 1800 model was introduced – the twin carburettor 'S'.

The Mini 1275S gave way to the less aggressive 1275 GT in 1969, two years after the entire Mini range had been updated with Mark II models. These were essentially similar to the earlier cars, but had a larger glass area, and the option of the 998cc engine as already used in the Riley Elf and Wolseley Hornet (which were discontinued in 1969).

Also in 1969, the Mini Clubman was introduced with the 998cc power unit and a slightly different body shell which featured an extended bonnet line and front wings and concealed door hinges.

For 1970 the Mini was given individual-make status. The Clubman gained the 48bhp 1098cc A Series engine for 1975, and the Mini's 848cc unit finally disappeared in 1980, to be universally replaced by the 998cc engine.

The early 1970s saw the introduction of a new front-wheel-drive saloon – the 1973

three-door (and, later, five-door) Metro hatchback, developed from Mini design but featuring gas suspension. Power was from A-Plus Series engines of 998cc or 1275cc capacity.

Despite competition from the Metro and many other modern small cars, the Mini continued to sell well during the 1980s, special-edition models and its anachronistic styling broadening its appeal.

The Princess was developed into the hatchback Ambassador range from March 1982, the top-of-the-range model being the Vanden Plas.

A new five-door hatchback, the Maestro, appeared in March 1983, with a choice of 1275cc A-Plus, or overhead-camshaft 1598cc R-Series engines.

In April 1984 a new Austin saloon – the Montego – was introduced, with 1275cc (A-Plus) 1598cc (overhead-camshaft S-Series) or 1993cc (O-Series) engines. The S-Series engine was fitted to Maestros from July 1984.

Above: Metro GTi, 16V launched in May 1990
Right: 1990 diesel-engined Maestro

Below: The Mini, still being built over 30 years after its launch
Below right: Montego saloon, popular with the fleet market

Allegro, to replace the 1100/1300 range. The Allegro was available with a choice of 1.1- or 1.3-litre (A Series) or 1.5- or 1.7-litre (E-Series) engines.

In 1975 the wedge-shaped Princess saloons were introduced. The initial choice of engine was between the 1798cc B-Series or 2227cc E-Series units. From July 1978 the overhead-camshaft O-Series engines were fitted, in 1695cc or 1993cc forms.

The next all-new Austin was the

Austin-Healey

Great Britain
1953–1971

Cornishman Donald Healey was interested in motoring and motor sport from an early age. After being invalided out of the Royal Flying Corps in 1917, he set up his own garage, before building a successful career in the motor industry. He started work with Riley in 1931.

In the meantime he had already achieved a number of successes in trials and rallying, and his participation in major events continued throughout the 1930s.

Healey hatched his ideas of producing his own car during World War II, and a prototype Healey was produced in 1945, at the Benford factory in Warwick. The 2.4-litre Riley-powered car had coil-spring/trailing-arm suspension, torque-tube transmission and, in production form, a choice of saloon or open two-seater bodywork. The saloon version was, in fact, the fastest production saloon in the world at the time, having a top speed of nearly 105mph (168km/h).

The model was developed from its original A-type, through B-, C-, D-, E- and F-types, until 1951.

As a result of co-operation between Healey and the American Nash-Kelvinator company, a new model – the Nash-Healey – was introduced in 1950, using a 3.8–litre six-cylinder Nash power unit. A restyled version with a 4.1-litre engine was also produced.

In 1951, a G-type convertible was produced, fitted with a three-litre Alvis engine.

By the end of the same year Donald Healey and his son Geoffrey had decided to produce a new sports car, and they approached Austin, who duly provided the engine and running gear – all from the A90 Atlantic, powered by a four-cylinder 2.7-litre overhead-valve unit. The Gerry

Above: 100 BN2, unveiled in 1952

Below: First 'Frogeye' Sprite

Above: Last of the big Healeys was the 1959 3000

Coker-styled car – the Healey 100 – had two-seater bodywork, and this fast, sleek model made its debut at the 1952 Earls Court Motor Show.

B.M.C. – under Leonard Lord – adopted the design, and the production car became the Austin-Healey 100 from 1953. Changes were later made to the transmission, including the fitting of a

four-speed gearbox. The aluminium-bodied, disc-braked 100S model arrived in 1955, as did the 100M, with a Le Mans specification engine.

The 100 Six model was introduced in 1956, fitted with B.M.C.'s six-cylinder

Right: Known originally simply as the Healey 100, the Austin-Healey 100 was introduced at the 1952 Earls Court Motor Show. The car took its four-cylinder overhead-valve engine and running gear from the Austin A90 Atlantic saloon.

C-Type engine of 2.6 litres and producing 102bhp. The car was developed into the 2.9-litre Austin-Healey 3000 of 1959, this model giving 124bhp and a top speed of nearly 120mph (193km/h). A triple-carburettor 132bhp Mark II version was introduced in 1961, and this continued in production, with minor modifications, until 1967, when the last so-called 'Big Healey' was built.

In the meantime, Austin-Healey had produced its small two-seater sports car, the Sprite, launched in May 1958. The car, designed by Geoffrey Healey and Gerry Coker, cleverly used many of the running gear components of the then-current Austin A35, including the front suspension, engine and transmission. Morris Minor-type rack-and-pinion steering was employed.

The engine was uprated by the use of twin carburettors to develop 43bhp (34bhp in the A35), giving a top speed of 85mph (136km/h). The distinctive styling of the original Sprite included headlamps mounted on top of the bonnet, giving rise to the universally adopted nickname of 'Frogeye'.

The Sprite was updated in 1961, the Mark II versions sharing restyled, flatter bodywork with the new M.G. Midget. The 948cc engine was retained, a higher compression ratio allowing it to produce another 6bhp. B.M.C.'s 1098cc A-Series engine, developing 56bhp, was fitted in 1963, and disc brakes were now employed at the front.

The specification was again revised in early 1964; the Mark III cars featured wind-up side windows, a new dashboard and semi-elliptic rear springs instead of the previous quarter-elliptics.

The last Austin-Healey Sprite was the Mark IV. Introduced for 1967, the new model was powered by a 65bhp version of the 1275cc A-Series engine, giving a top speed of well over 90mph (145km/h). The last Austin-Healey Sprite was built in 1971, although the similar M.G. Midgets continued in production.

Above: 1958 100/6 with C-type engine

Below: 1958 Sprite with 948cc engine

Above: 1963 ex-works 3000 Mk III

Below: 1967 ex-works Sprite in racing trim

Austro-Daimler

Austria
1899–1936

In 1899 the Vienna company, Bierenz-Fischer & Co., agreed to build 100 Daimler cars a year under licence from the German manufacturer in Cannstatt. Production from this new company, Österreichische Daimler Motoren AG, was poor, however, resulting in Daimler's son Paul being sent to organize matters in 1902.

Above: 1909 Austro-Daimler charabanc

Following this the Austrian company separated from its parent (although full financial independence was not achieved until 1906) and in 1903 Ferdinand Porsche took over as director. Porsche was full of new ideas but these took time to put into operation, and the company agreed to build the unexciting Maja cars for Emile Jellinek, consul-general of the Austro-Hungarian Empire in Nice. This

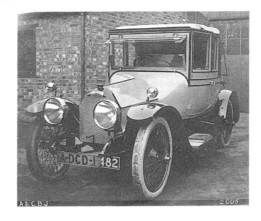

Above: 25/30hp Austro-Daimler tourer

continued until 1914.

In the meantime, Porsche introduced a couple of well-made standard designs until his 1910 Prince Henry Tour winner, of the same name, gave the company an international reputation. All links with the German firm were then dropped and the cars officially took on the name Austro-Daimler in 1911. It was that same year that a Porsche-designed car won the Austrian Alpine Tour, and by the outbreak of World War I the Vienna firm was Austria's biggest car manufacturer.

During the war Austro-Daimler made military vehicles, some of which were

Below: The first new post-war Austro-Daimler fast tourer, the 1921 AD 617, was powered by a six-cylinder 4.4-litre single-overhead-cam engine.

Above: c. 1919 Sascha racing voiturette

interchangeable between road and railway, and afterwards a number of the earlier cars were assembled in Liège from pre-war parts as Alfa-Legias. As well as reworking some of the pre-war designs, Austro-Daimler introduced some exciting fast tourers which were also successful in motor sport.

Unhappy, Porsche returned to Daimler in 1923, being replaced by Karl Rabe. In 1925 Austro-Daimler became connected with Austro-Fiat, also of Vienna, then three years later it merged with Puch-Werke to become Austro-Daimler-Puchwerke.

By 1935 that company's six-year association with Steyr-Werke, and the similarity between the two products, lead their joint bankers to force an amalgamation as Steyr-Daimler-Puch. By the following year the Austro-Daimler name had disappeared.

Above: 1931 4.6-litre ADR8

Ballot

France
1919–1933

Ernest Ballot gained his engineering experience with the merchant marine, founding Ballot et Cie in Paris in 1906 to build marine engines. By the outbreak of war in 1914 he had expanded into cars, producing commercial and competition engines for Delage, Mass and La Licorne, having formed the Etablissements Ballot in 1910. Ballot was administration director of this company, with financial backing coming from people such as Adolphe Clément, Fernand Charron and Pierre Forgeot, the last-named a future government minister.

Above: 1922 two-litre Grand Prix car
Left: 1924 overhead-camshaft 2LT tourer

The first of Ballot's own racing cars, equipped with an eight-cylinder engine of 4.9-litres capacity, appeared at the end of World War I for the 1919 Indianapolis 500 race. It was designed by Ernest Henry, famous for his pre-war competition Peugeots. In 1921 Henry designed a three-litre car for Ballot especially for the French Grand Prix, and Ballot also developed a two-litre four-cylinder racer. A limited number of purely road-going vehicles, based on that car and with extraordinary performance, soon followed. The same year a more practical fast tourer was also produced, almost unique in France at that time.

Three years later a tuned tourer was offered, this designed by Henry's successor, Fernand Vadier, who had left Panhard to join Ballot's marine-diesel department just after the war. Vadier himself left Ballot in 1926 to sell Dewandre servo-operated brakes to the car manufacturing industry.

A six-cylinder car appeared in 1927, with a 2.6-litre straight-eight being launched at that year's Paris Salon, Ballot's first of that design since his Grand Prix cars of 1921. This was further developed into a three-litre car in 1930, but unfortunately by then the Depression had

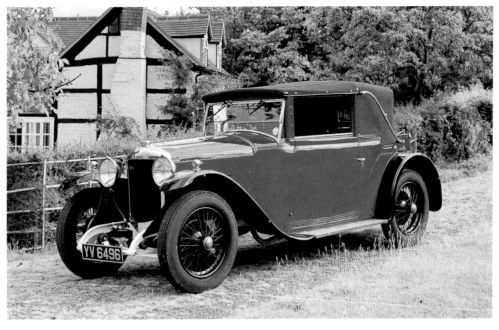

Above: 1926 2LT saloon

Above: 1928 2LTS

Below: 2.6-litre straight-eight RH saloon

reduced the demand for such vehicles. Sales slumped, Ballot was fired by Forgeot and the company was taken over by Hispano-Suiza in 1930. A Ballot chassis was used with a Hispano-Suiza engine for the Junior, which was produced in the old Ballot works until their closure in 1933.

Below: The 2LS, Ballot's first road-going car, was developed from a straight-eight racer, built for the French Grand Prix in 1921. It was fitted with brakes on all wheels.

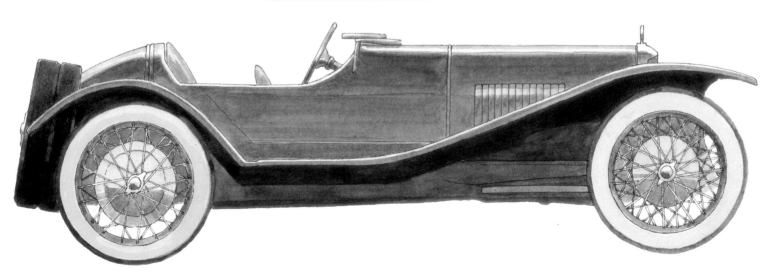

Bentley

Great Britain
1921 to date

Walter Owen Bentley started out as a railway apprentice, but progressed to racing motorcycles and then to distributing the French D.F.P. car in London. Successful modifications he designed for the D.F.P. persuaded him to design his own car in 1919, and the four-cylinder three-litre Bentley entered production in 1921.

Over the next ten years, the Bentley name signified expensive and powerful cars; the four-cylinder 4½-litre and its limited-production supercharged derivative in 1927 continued the line of sporting models, while the 1925 six-cylinder 6½-litre and its eight-litre successor of 1930 were designed for the carriage trade.

Below: The Bentley Super Sports, a variant of the legendary 3-litre model, had a distinctive tapering radiator. Its four-cylinder engine could take it up to 160km/h (100mph), but its handling was uncertain and only a few were built.

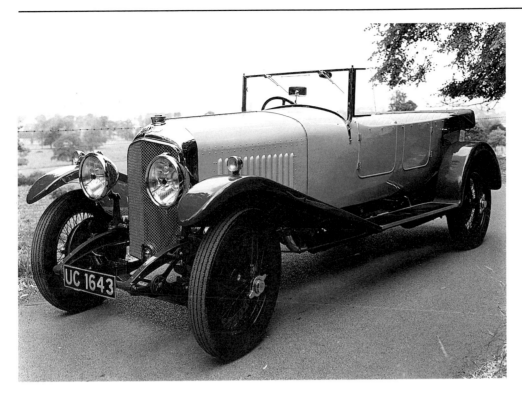

Bentley sales hard, however. In 1931, the company slid into receivership and was bought by Rolls-Royce.

The first new Bentley, built at the Rolls-Royce factory in Derby rather than Bentley's earlier Cricklewood, London, home, was the the 1933 3½-litre. This 'Silent Sports Car' was very different from the huge and muscular Bentleys which had gone before, having a tuned version of the contemporary Rolls-Royce 20/25 engine in a new chassis frame. When the 20/25 became a 25/30 in 1936, the Bentley followed suit and took the larger engine to become a 4¼-litre. When World War II put an end to production, Bentley had just introduced a new model called the Mark V, but only a handful were built.

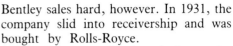

Above left: 1925 Bentley three-litre tourer

Above: 1927 4½-litre
Right: Eight-litre in-line six saloon
Below: Gurney Nutting-bodied 3½-litre
Bottom: 1938 model with 4½-litre chassis

Only the curiously undistinguished four-litre model of 1930 failed to enhance the marque's reputation.

Bentleys scored numerous racing and record-breaking successes, most notably five wins at Le Mans. But the cars were built in only small numbers and the cost of the racing programme was high. Massive losses in 1924 were followed by liquidation and reorganization of the company in 1925, and only the intervention of the millionaire sportsman and Bentley racing driver Woolf Barnato put the company back on its feet. The Depression which followed the Wall Street Crash in 1929 hit

Below: 1928 Bentley, 1961 Glidden Tour

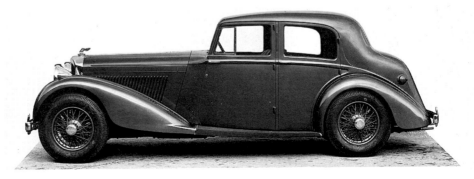

Like Rolls-Royce, Bentley had only ever offered chassis before 1946, leaving bodywork to the customer's choice of coachbuilder. Careful rationalization for the post-war range, however, saw the Mark VI introduced with a 'standard-steel' saloon body made by Pressed Steel. Now built at Crewe, the post-war Bentleys were largely badge-engineered Rolls-Royce models (and their characteristics will be found under the entry for Rolls-Royce). All were made in far smaller numbers than their Rolls-Royce equivalents.

Nevertheless, there were always some differences between the ranges. Thus, Bentley never offered a large limousine model, and there was never a Rolls-Royce equivalent of the fabulous R-type

Below: The 1946 standard-bodied Mark VI

Above: The stunning 1951 S1 Continental
Below: 1953 R-type Continental

Below: One of the last cars to be built before the company's collapse and takeover by Rolls-Royce was a four-cylinder sports car, the 4½-litre.

Continental introduced in 1952. Continental versions of the S-type introduced in 1955 had better performance than the standard models, but there was none of the Bentley sporting heritage evident in them.

After 1982, Bentley was revitalized as a separate marque through new models for which there was no direct Rolls-Royce equivalent: the Eight and the Mulsanne Turbo, for example, both derived from the Roll-Royce Silver Spirit first seen in 1980. The revised Turbo R model for 1985 indicated the way Bentley would go in the future, blending the sumptuous luxury of Crewe's best with very high performance and superb handling; a return, in fact, to the Bentley characteristics of the 1920s and 1930s.

Above: The T-series, the first monocoque
Below: The turbo 1989 Bentley Eight

Bentley went further to separate its range from that of Rolls-Royce with the introduction of the Continental R in 1991. This two-door coupé version of the Turbo R helped to rebuild the company's image as a manufacturer of high-quality sporting vehicles. The name, too, conjured up memories of one of the greatest post-war grand touring Bentleys, the Continental R of 1952. Rolls-Royce offered no two-door car in their own range.

The car's sporting appeal was further enhanced with a smaller version of the Continental, named the Continental T, launched in 1996. With a shorter wheelbase, svelte looks and an extra 16bhp from the 6.75-litre V8, it was a car to appeal to the younger Bentley owner, if there is such a thing.

In the meantime, the company had also brought out a convertible version of the Continental, called the Azure, Bentley's most expensive car. Heavyweight boxer, Mike Tyson was reported to have bought no fewer than four Azures at $319,000 apiece from a Las Vegas dealer.

Top right: The 1997 Bentley Turbo R

Middle Right: The two-door Continental T

Below: 1997 Bentley Brooklands R

Above: The Azure was Bentley's only convertible during the 1990s

Below: The Continental T had the most powerful engine in the range at 405bhp

Benz

Germany
1885–1926

The engine for the 1885 Tricycle was a single-cylinder four-stroke of one horsepower, producing a maximum speed of 16km/h (10mph).

Benz continued experimenting and refining this invention for the next five years, and began limited car production in 1890. He was joined in that year by two partners who relieved him of the responsibility for sales and administration, leaving him free to deal with technical innovation. This permitted rapid progress

Karl Benz had worked as a young man for a Stuttgart carriage builder, but the burgeoning gas-engine industry tempted him to design his own two-stroke stationary engine and to join a modest but established stationary-engine enterprise. His next step was to secure financial backing and to set up on his own in the stationary-engine business in Mannheim.

Benz soon became interested in combining his knowledge of the carriage trade with his expertise in stationary engines to build a self-propelled vehicle. Using petrol instead of gas as fuel, he built his first car – generally considered to have been the first in the world – in 1885.

Above: Model 3 vis-à-vis *car*
Below: 1892 Benz Viktoria

Below: 1901 single-cylinder sports

from the original three-wheeled designs to a four-wheeler called the Viktoria in 1891, and four years later Benz developed a van and bus from the basic design. Meanwhile, the technical advances of the expensive Viktoria had been adapted to a much cheaper model known as the Velo and introduced in 1894. This was the world's first series-production car.

The company continued to introduce new models and by the end of the decade it had built 2,000 cars and had a production capacity of 600 cars a year. In addition, it had sales agencies in several far-flung countries. All this was sufficient to make the Benz company the world's leading motor manufacturer at the turn of the century. Yet Benz himself was a man of conservative disposition, and his designs rapidly became outmoded as motor-car development progressed by leaps and bounds. In an attempt to halt the resulting sales decline, Benz's sales director engaged another designer to build a new model which went on sale in 1902. This provoked a rift: Benz left his own company a year later, was persuaded to rejoin briefly in 1905, but then left for good in 1906.

Above: 1894 rear-engined Velo
Below: 1895 Benz omnibus

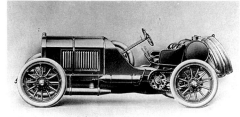

Above: 1908 four-cylinder Grand Prix car
Left: 1903 twin-cylinder Sport-Phaeton
Below left: 1905-7 four-cylinder tourer

This left the ailing company under the guidance of its chief engineer, Hans Nibel, who believed that motor racing would both lead to technical improvements and gather the publicity which would restore the Benz fortunes. A comeback began in 1907, and by 1909 sufficient technical progress had been made for the company to build the 200bhp Blitzen-Benz, which broke the World Land Speed Record that year and held it until 1922.

Under Nibel, the Benz company introduced a wide range of road cars, which sold to an increasingly broad market, and in 1914 it introduced its first six-cylinder model. Wartime saw the inevitable concentration on trucks and

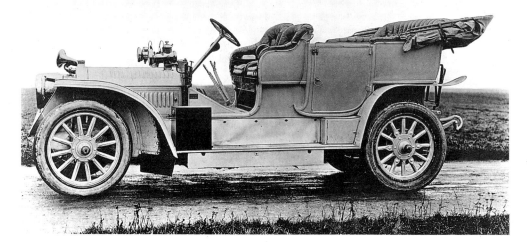

Right: 1918 6/18 had a four-cylinder ohc engine
Below: The 1909 Blitzen-Benz was powered by a 21,495cc four-cylinder Benz airship engine developing 200bhp at 1300rpm.

aero-engines, but when peace returned in 1918 the Benz company faced problems. Germany's economy had been shattered, and the car market was slow to recover. Although there were brave attempts at publicity through racing – notably with the rear-engined Tropfenwagen of 1923 – the road cars were mainly conventional vehicles derived from a 1914 design.

Germany was gripped by serious inflation after 1923, and it rapidly became apparent that either the Benz company or its rivals at Daimler would go under. In 1924, the two companies reached a co-operative agreement, and in 1926 they merged as the Daimler-Benz Aktiengesellschaft (see *Mercedes-Benz*).

Left: 1909-13 four-cylinder 14/30   *Above: 1923 Tropfenwagen Grand Prix*

Berliet

France
1895–1939

The firm of Berliet, based in Lyon, France, began producing cars as early as 1895. Small numbers were produced in the early years, but the cars were advanced for their time, with wheel-controlled steering and four-speed gearboxes. Power came from a rear-mounted engine.

Right: 1901 Type B with chain drive
Far right: 1908 Double Phaeton

Below: A post World War One four-cylinder sidevalve-engined car producing 16hp.

In 1901 the firm of Audibert-Lavirotte came under Berliet's wing, and the range of cars was enlarged – two- and four-cylinder models were now available.

Berliet concentrated on large cars for several years from 1902, producing, for example, 40hp (6.3-litre), 60hp (8.6-litre) and 80hp (11-litre) models. Berliets of this period were built on pressed-steel chassis and many featured overhead inlet valves. Indeed, they were similar in concept and layout to the grand Mercedes of the period.

Shaft-drive chassis were available from 1907, and Berliet offered a wide range of models until the outbreak of World War I, with engines ranging from small twin-cylinder units to very large sixes.

After the war the company built sidevalve-engined four-cylinder cars,

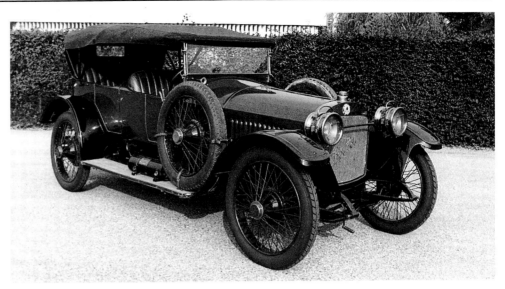

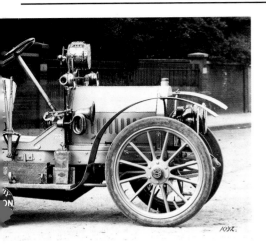

Above: 1906 22hp car
Below: 1919 overhead-valve Berliet VB

although by the mid-1920s innovative features such as four-speed gearboxes, front-wheel brakes and overhead valves were appearing in the specifications of some Berliets, notably the 1200cc 10/20 and the four-litre 23/70 models.

The late 1920s saw a mixture of sidevalve- and overhead-valve engines being used, in capacities ranging from 1.5 litres (four cylinders) to 4.1 litres (six cylinders).

In 1933 came the introduction of the 1600cc 9CV (or, optionally, two-litre 11CV) Type 944, with American-influenced styling. Deluxe models had independent front suspension, while overhead- or sidevalve-engine options were available initially.

The last Berliet saloon was the Dauphine, built from 1936. Chassis design was advanced, with rack-and-pinion steering, independent front suspension and a synchromesh gearbox. As World War II approached, Berliet bought bodies from Peugeot, so the last Dauphines had

Peugeot 402 bodywork.

No Berliet cars were produced after the war, although the company was already – and continues to be – a highly successful commercial vehicle manufacturer.

Above: 1911 four-cylinder 22hp car
Below left: 1923 Model VI
Below: 1936 2-litre Dauphine
Bottom: The last Berliet car was a 1937 2-litre Dauphine

Bignan

France
1919–1931

Although Jacques Bignan first collaborated with Lucien Picker in 1911 to set up an engine firm at Courbevoie, Paris, their first completed car under the Bignan name did not appear until 1919. This was the 17CV, a big 3½-litre tourer which was actually produced in the Grégoire factory at Poissy, on a de la Fournaise chassis frame.

The 17CV's sidevalve engine was designed by Nemorin Causan, who had worked on early Delage competition engines and for Corre La Licorne. Causan also assisted development of engines for Bignan's own racing entries. In Bignan's first event, the Grand Prix de Voiturettes in 1920, however, he raced in a 1400cc T-head four-cylinder car which he had designed himself in 1914. The two cars finished second and third.

The 17CV's engine was enlarged to three litres in 1921. This car was marketed in England as the Grégoire-Campbell, but ceased production in 1923.

The 2-litre 11CV appeared in 1922, and

this was to provide the basis for the future Bignan range. In that year the company also introduced its famous desmodromic-valve racer. This system, where the valves were both opened *and* closed positively by means of cams, was never as successful as the company anticipated, and was dropped in favour of a more orthodox arrangement, winning the Spanish Touring Car Grands Prix two years running.

Together, Bignan and Causan successfully extracted higher performances from sidevalve engines designed before World War I. Their reputation was for producing vehicles with the evocative Bignan grille but with relatively cheap mechanical components. Their cars of the early 1920s often used proprietary Ballot, S.C.A.P. and C.I.M.E. engines, but the sporting image was kept up.

In 1924 a Bignan two-litre tourer won the Monte Carlo Rally, and competition entry remained strong until 1927, when a lower placing in the Spanish Touring Car event was to mark the company's last attempt; although Bignan himself continued racing, winning the 1928 Monte Carlo Rally in a Fiat.

By 1926 Bignan's financial situation was dire but the company was kept going by a trust until 1931, producing a rebadged E.H.P. as the Bignan-M.O.P.

Below: 1922 2-litre racer

BMW

Germany
1928 to date

The Bayerische Motoren Werke AG began life in Munich as a manufacturer of aircraft engines, and turned to motor-cycle production in 1923. That year's shaft-drive R-32 model became hugely successful, and motor cycles remain a BMW strength today.

Above: 1898-1900 Decauville-Wartburg

In 1928 the company diversified into car manufacture by taking over Dixi, who were already building the British Austin Seven under licence at Einsenach. This model was rapidly developed, initially as the BMW 3/15, and by 1933 the company was confident enough to introduce a six-cylinder model with a stretched wheelbase which betrayed none of its Austin Seven ancestry. Within a year, the six-cylinder engine had reached a capacity of 1.5 litres and the mundane saloons and tourers had been complemented by a sporting model called the 315.

Above: 1922 Dixi with 1.5-litre engine

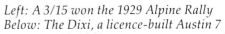

Left: A 3/15 won the 1929 Alpine Rally
Below: The Dixi, a licence-built Austin 7
Centre: 1933 AM4
Bottom: Special-bodied AM4 3/20

Above: 1933 303 with two doors
Below: The 1936 BMW 326 was powered
by a 1971cc 50hp engine, and was in direct
competition with the small Mercedes of the
period.

The engine size was increased to two litres in 1935, and this powered the 1936 326, which was the decade's most significant model. This had a new chassis and flowing styling, and was to sire all the BMWs of the late 1930s. These included the 328 two-seater sports car of 1937, which quickly became a significant force in European road-racing, and the attractively styled 327 coupés and convertibles. The last pre-war development was the 3½-litre 334 of 1939, but only a few were built. These BMWs of the late 1930s were sold in Britain as Frazer-Nash BMWs.

Top: 315 with 1490cc six-cylinder engine
Above: 1934 1.5-litre BMW Type 315

Above: The pre-war 315 roadster was capable of 100km/h (62mph)

BMW introduced the 328 in 1936. It set new standards in precision, roadholding and cornering, and took first place at the Nürburgring in June that year.

Left: 1939-41 335 saloon
Top: 1938 328, a much-admired sports car
Below: The 328 won the 1940 Mille Miglia

BMW hit serious difficulties after World War II, with its Munich factories bombed out and its Eisenach plant lost to East Germany. But motor-cycle production resumed in 1948, and booming sales financed the introduction of a new car in 1952: the 501 saloon. Its basic shape continued until 1964, gaining larger six-cylinder engines and a pair of V8s; and the drivetrains appeared after 1955 in sleek coupé models called 503s. Yet sales of all these expensive models, and of the excellent V8-engined 507 sports model of 1957 were slow. The money came from smaller BMWs, the Isetta bubble-car built under licence after 1955, and the rear-engined 700 after 1959.

Above: 1952 six-cylinder 501

Below: 1956 V-8 507 roadster

Below: Four-door state car on 501 chassis

Above: The V8-engined 502 arrived in 1955

Below: Produced from 1955 the BMW 507 was a truly beautiful car which could reach a top speed of 200km/h (124mph). It had a five-speed gear box and an optional self-locking differential.

It was the medium-sized 1500 saloon of 1961 which saved BMW from bankruptcy. This initiated a series of high-quality four-cylinder models over the next decade, with engines ranging from 80bhp in the 1500 to 170bhp in the limited-production Turbo 2002, while there were two-door, four-door, cabriolet, and (after 1971) hatchback 'Touring' bodies.

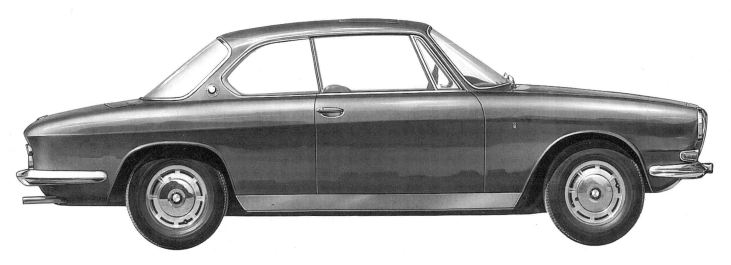

Top left: 700 Cabriolet boasted 40bhp
Left: 1960 BMW Isetta derived from Italian Iso

Top: 1962 1500cc four-door saloon
Above: Bertone-styled 1962 3200CS
Below: 2002 Turbo offered 170bhp

The success of this range made the acquisition of extra production capacity necessary and, in 1967, BMW bought the Glas company, into whose factory it expanded after a year or so of making modified Glas coupés as BMW 1600GTs. Meanwhile, the big coupé line was continued after 1965 by Bertone-styled models, and a six-cylinder engine arrived in 1968 to power a new range of larger saloons and a face-lifted coupé. By 1971, this engine had been stretched to three litres for both ranges, and to 3.2 litres for the saloons.

Above: 1971 2002 ti1 offered luxury with performance

For the 1970s and 1980s, BMW rationalized its model ranges. The '3' series would be medium-sized saloons, the '5' series executive saloons, the '7' series luxury saloons, and the '6' series big sporting coupés. Engines from 1.6 litres to 3.5 litres allowed a large choice of models.

Top: 1974 225km/h (140mph) 3.0 CSi
Above: 1971 2500 luxury saloon

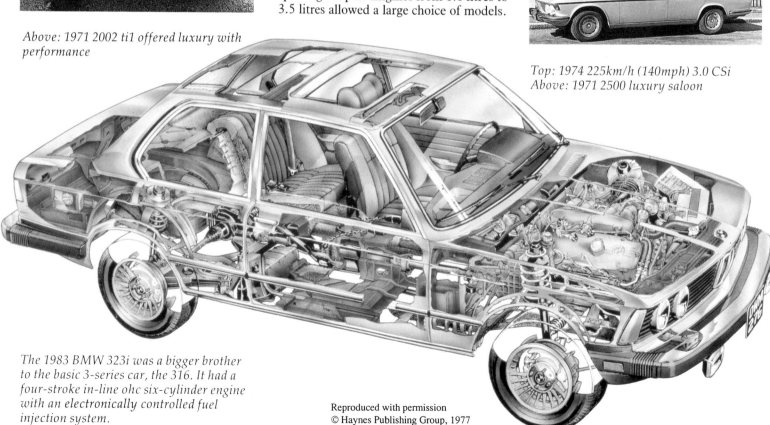

The 1983 BMW 323i was a bigger brother to the basic 3-series car, the 316. It had a four-stroke in-line ohc six-cylinder engine with an electronically controlled fuel injection system.

Reproduced with permission
© Haynes Publishing Group, 1977

High-performance versions marketed under the Alpina banner after 1978, plus the 260km/h (162mph) mid-engined M1 coupé of 1979, promoted a sporting image. So too did the success of BMW's 1.5-litre turbocharged Formula One engine, which propelled Nelson Piquet's Brabham to the world driver's crown in 1981 and 1983, and the marketing of 'M' cars (M3, M5, M535i, M635 Csi) which were built by BMW's Motorsport department.

Right and below: Two views of this fast mid-engine sports car, the BMW M1
Bottom: The 528i executive express

Above: 1983 two-door 323i
Left: 628 CSi coupé
Below: 732i four-door saloon

An internal rival to this department, the BMW Technik think-tank division, designed and produced the Z1 two-seat sports car which went on sale in 1989. Meant to continue the tradition of low-volume high-technology roadsters established by the 328 and 507, it employs the 170bhp 2.5-litre straight-six engine of the 325i.

Above: 1990 8-series coupé

BMW's most significant move as it prepared for the 1990s was the introduction of all-new '5', '7' and '8' series cars (the latter replacing the '6'). The '5' was instantly acclaimed for its well-sorted chassis and refinement; the top-line '7', the 750iL with its 300bhp 5.0-litre V12, presented a convincing challenge to German market leader Mercedes-Benz; and the similarly powered 850i 2+2-seater sports coupé, artificially limited to 250km/h (155mph) but capable of 274km/h (170mph) emphasized BMW's determination to achieve technical supremacy over Mercedes.

Based around the company's outstanding 170bhp six-cylinder engine from the 325i, the sleek Z1 has scintillating performance and superb handling.

A new 3-series arrived for 1990. Initially available only in four-door saloon form, the new car had smoother, more contemporary lines and featured the Z-axle rear suspension developed on the Z1 roadster. Engines remained the same, with a choice of four- and six-cylinder units from 1.6 to 2.5 litres. BMW followed the saloon with a two-door coupé in 1992, and in the same year brought out a new sporting M3 with a 286bhp 3.0-litre engine and later a 321bhp 3.2-litre version, making it one of the fastest production BMWs ever built. The range was further expanded with cabriolet and touring (estate) models, as well as a new hatchback version called the Compact.

The old 2.5-litre in-line six engine was replaced in 1995 for a new more efficient and lighter alloy 2.8-litre version. The 2.8 possessed plenty of low-down torque making the 3 series a very relaxed and swift car.

The often-forgotten but highly competent 5-series range was expanded with the introduction of the four-wheel-drive 525ix Touring – a useful go-anywhere load carrier

Above: The M3 was a true status symbol of the 1990s and gave 321bhp

Below: The 3-series Compact provided a cheap entry-level car for younger buyers

Above: The M3 Evolution was also available in four-door form from 1995

with fine road manners. New V8 engines became available in 1992, in 3- and 4-litre forms. These new power units displaced the larger capacity straight-six motors. The 5-series was completely revamped for the end of 1995 to much acclaim from the motoring press. Some magazines even described it as the greatest car in the world. It was certainly the finest car available in its class.

The luxurious 7-series received its face-lift in 1994 and gained the new 3.5- and 4.5-litre V8 engines in 1996. Despite its advanced technical specification, high performance and fine chassis, the 8 -series was never a big seller. A smaller V8-engined derivative helped sales a little, due to a lower price and similar performance to the V12-

Above: The 5-series estate was available from 1991. This is a 1997 model

Right: The 3-series Touring didn't offer as much space as many rivals but still sold well

engined version.

A high price had also adversely affected the Z1 sports car, forcing BMW to bring production to an end in the early 1990s. But the company had not given up on the sports car yet. In 1995 the Z3 was launched. It was based on the 3-series compact, meaning it didn't even carry the Z-axle its name suggested and was initially available with either a 1.8- or 1.9-litre engine. Cries for more power soon led to the introduction of a 2.8-litre model and later a fire-breathing M3-engined version.

The Z3 was the first car to be built in BMW's new American factory, based at Spartanburg, South Carolina.

Top: The 5-series was updated in 1997 and set new standards of refinement

Right: The V12-engined 850 was joined by the cheaper V8 840 in 1993

Above: The new 3-series convertible proved to be just as popular as it predecessor

Left: The Z3 was initially only available with four-cylinder engine

In 1994 BMW bought the British company, Rover, and the valuable Land-Rover subsidiary, from owners British Aerospace. The company also announced that it would lend its expertise to Rolls-Royce to help develop two new engines.

Right: BMW's top-end saloon, the 7-series, was available with a 5.4-litre V12 engine

Below: After the launch of the Z3, BMW announced there was a coupé version on the drawing board

Léon Bollée

France
1895–1933

Léon Bollée's interest in motor cars began with his father, Amédée Sr., who pioneered steam-powered road-going vehicles, and also his brother, Amédée Jr., who joined his father's firm.

Léon set up on his own, producing his first small petrol-driven car in 1895. It was he who named this machine a *voiturette*, literally 'little car', which soon became the accepted term for vehicles of this type. It was manufactured by various firms for the next four years, when Bollée followed it with a less-successful larger vehicle, causing the marque to disappear from the market between 1901 and 1903.

Bollée then returned with two more powerful, expensive cars financially

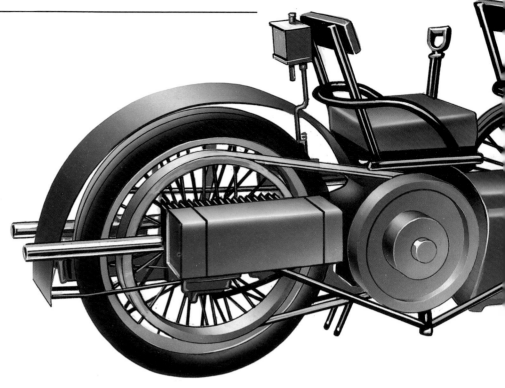

Below: Bollée steam carriage, c. 1880

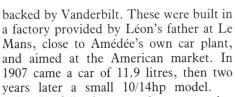

Left: Léon Bollée named his small two-seater car of 1895 'voiturette'. The 650cc, 3hp three-wheeler featured hot tube ignition, three-speed transmission, and belt drive. It was a fast machine for its time, and was capable of more than 48km/h (30mph).

Mans factory was sold to Sir William Morris in 1924. Automobiles Léon Bollée became Morris Motors Ltd., Usines Léon Bollée, and began producing more elegant Van Vestrant and Hans Landstad-designed versions of the current Morris range. Harry Smith was brought in from Morris's engine branch to become the new works' manager.

By the end of the 1920s, however, the Morris-run operation was making six-figure losses and sales had plummeted. With the onset of the Depression the company pulled out in 1931, selling the factory to Société Nouvelle Léon Bollée, a syndicate containing Harry Smith and A. Dunlop Mackenzie, and in which one of the main component suppliers had an interest.

This was not a success, with just a few cars and commercials being produced, and lasted for only two years, folding in 1933.

Below: c. 1910 Léon Bollée chassis
Bottom: The four-seater, four-door Léon Bollée Type M of 1926

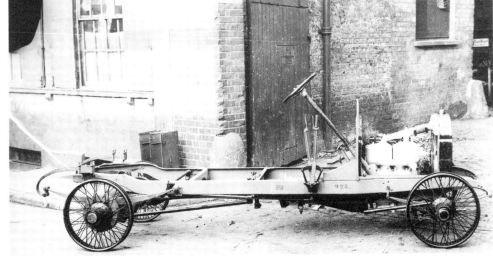

backed by Vanderbilt. These were built in a factory provided by Léon's father at Le Mans, close to Amédée's own car plant, and aimed at the American market. In 1907 came a car of 11.9 litres, then two years later a small 10/14hp model.

By the following year there were nine cars in the range and between 150 and 350 were being produced per year. In 1913 Léon Bollée met an early death, with control of car manufacturing falling to his widow.

After World War I the marque became increasingly old-fashioned, and the Le

Brasier

France
1897–1930

Georges Richard's firm, based in Paris, initially produced electrical meters and photographic and optical equipment, and had already been established for over 45 years when it produced its first car. This was in 1897, and it took the form of a simple, Benz-inspired vehicle.

By 1900, however, Société Anonyme Georges Richard, run by Georges and his brother Max, was producing Vivinus cars under licence from Belgium, although they were badged under the Richard name.

New investment in the Richard firm from the Franco-Swiss Indusmine company enabled it to build a factory near the Panhard et Levassor works at Ivry-Port and employ 300 men. In 1901 a new vehicle appeared – Richard's first shaft-driven model – following the style of Renault and Darracq.

Also in 1901, designer Henri Brasier joined the company from Mors, producing a 14hp car with an Arbel steel frame for the

following year. Brasier introduced little that was new and although four new cars were introduced in 1902, badged as Richard-Brasiers, they were nothing startling and very much resembled other makes of the period.

In 1904 and 1905 two Brasier-designed

vehicles won the Gordon Bennett Trophy for France races, but 1905 saw the withdrawal of Georges Richard from the company, leaving Brasier in charge. The firm became first *Trèfle a Quatre Feuilles* ('Four Leaf Clover') after its badge, then Brasier, then Automobiles Brasier, and

Above: 1903 Richard-Brasier 24hp Wagonette

Below: The 14hp Richard-Brasier tourer of 1905 was a chain-driven, four-seater
Right: 1914 Brasier 24hp six-cylinder

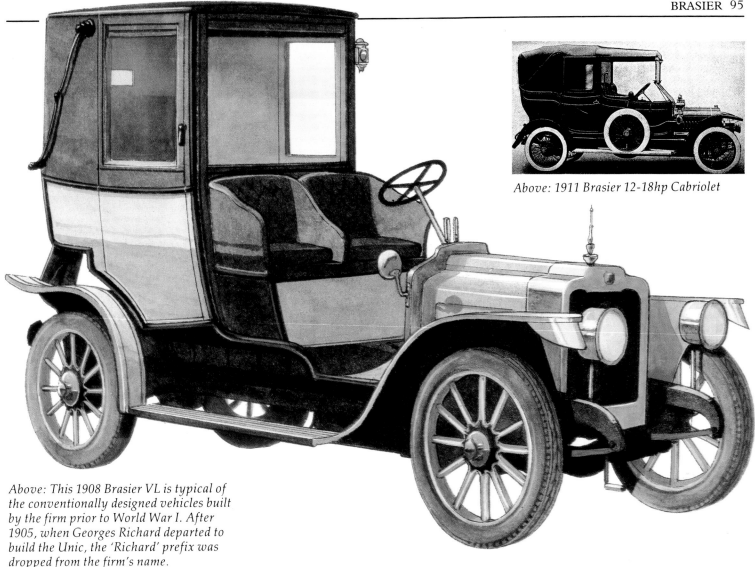

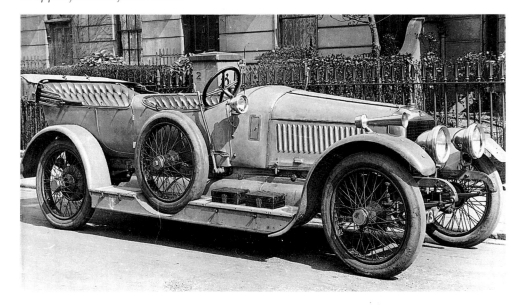

Above: 1911 Brasier 12-18hp Cabriolet

Above: This 1908 Brasier VL is typical of the conventionally designed vehicles built by the firm prior to World War I. After 1905, when Georges Richard departed to build the Unic, the 'Richard' prefix was dropped from the firm's name.

cars were even made under licence in Italy as Fides.

Until World War I, Brasier cars were unexcitingly conventional, with the exception of a modern light car introduced in 1912. During the hostilities commercial vehicles were continued and the company also built Hispano-Suiza aero-engines.

After the war Brasier continued to produce expensive four-cylinder cars, but demand was failing. Reorganization in 1926 led to the company becoming Chaigneau-Brasier and two years later it introduced a car which was of too unusual a design and far too costly for the period to sell well. Georges Irat's son Michel then took over, producing cars under that name until the factory closed in 1930 and was eventually bought by Delahaye.

Bristol

Great Britain 1947 to date

The Bristol has always been an individualistic and expensive high-performance car. After World War II, the Bristol Aeroplane Company found itself with surplus engineering capacity and skill; under Sir George White, it turned these to the small-scale manufacture of aircraft-quality motor cars. Bristol's association with BMW's U.K. importers, AFN Ltd., ensured that the first model – the 1947 400 – had an engine and some styling features derived from the pre-war Type 328 BMW.

The 401 was introduced in 1948, with a more aerodynamic body built under Superleggera Touring patents, and a drop-head 402 version followed. In 1953 came the 403 and 404, the former a more powerful version of the 401 and the latter a handsome, short-wheelbase, fixed-head two-plus-two coupé which quickly became known as the Businessman's Express. The 406 of 1954 offered the 404's styling but with four doors on the longer-wheelbase chassis.

With minor but effective face-lifts, the styling introduced for the 1957 406 saloon served until the demise of the 1969 411 in 1978. The old BMW-derived engine had reached the limit of its development long before this, however, and the 1961 407 was the first Bristol to use a modified Canadian Chrysler V8 engine with automatic transmission. Meanwhile, car manufacture had been separated from that of aircraft, and Bristol Cars Ltd. was set up in 1961 under Sir George White and former racing driver Tony Crook. Crook took sole control in 1973.

New styling arrived with the 1978 603 saloon, and Italian Gianni Zagato styled the 412 Targa-top model, which became the turbocharged Beaufighter in 1980. Still with anachronistic separate-chassis construction and distinctive styling derived from the 603, the range continued after 1982 with the Britannia saloon, the turbocharged Brigand and the export-only Beaufort.

Above: 1949 drophead Bristol 402

Above: 1950 Bristol 400

Above: 1958 Bristol 404

Above: Bristol Type 411, introduced 1969

Above: 1978 Bristol 603 V8

B.S.A.

Great Britain 1907–1940

Better known in the world of motor cycling, B.S.A. (British Small Arms) had a reputation before World War I for cars of simplicity and low cost, some of them boasting front-wheel drive.

The company originated in 1861 in Small Heath, Birmingham, making guns. Its well-known 'piled arms' trademark was adopted in 1880 when applied to the Otto Dicycle which was, in fact, a tricycle. Its first car, a copy of the 40hp Italia, was introduced in 1908.

In 1910 the company made the first wholly B.S.A. motor-cycle and acquired Daimler, Britain's first car manufacturer. From 1911 B.S.A. effectively made scaled-down Daimlers with sleeve-valve engines.

After World War I the company introduced the vee-twin Ten which was built until 1924, being outlived by the sleeve-valve car which lasted until 1926.

The vee-twin returned in 1929 to power a front-wheel-drive three-wheeler which acquired a fourth wheel in 1932. The vehicle became more of a 'proper' car the following year when a four-cylinder engine was fitted.

After a year-long break in production manufacture recommenced in 1935 when the car was christened the B.S.A. Scout. It remained in production until 1940 when B.S.A. reverted to munitions and military vehicles to help the war effort led by chief executive James Leek.

During the war the Scout light reconnaissance car and the heavier Daimler Mark I armoured car – B.S.A. had anticipated the war – excelled in their military duties, and the factory was able to claim that not a single major modification was necessary to cope with all theatres of war.

When the war ended in 1945, the Daimler division of B.S.A. resumed production while B.S.A. decided to concentrate on two-wheelers, soon becoming world leaders in this field.

B.S.A.'s war-time Scout featured four-wheel drive from a central differential, fluid-flywheel transmission and a 2.5-litre Daimler engine. It was designed to reach 60mph (96km/h) in forward gear and 55mph (88km/h) in reverse, with steering at both ends and independent suspension. The vehicle was conceived in 1938 at the request of the War Office and B.S.A. staff worked with the Wheeled Vehicles Experimental Department at Farnborough on the project. Only 152cm (60in) high, the armoured vehicle excelled in the desert, where Rommel even made his escape in a captured Scout.

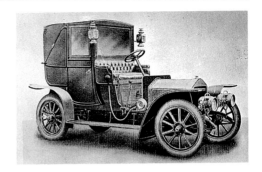

Top: 1910 18/23hp Single Landaulette

Below left: 1914 13.9hp B.S.A.

Below: 1924 B.S.A. 'Ten'

Above: 1933 B.S.A. four-cylinder 'trike'

Above: 1935 B.S.A. Sports Coupé
Below: 1938 front-wheel-drive B.S.A. Scout

Bugatti

Germany
1909–1918
France
1918–1956

Ettore Bugatti showed a remarkable affinity for cars at a comparatively young age. Born in Milan, Italy, in 1881, he was successfully racing a twin-engined tricycle at the age of 18, and two years later he designed and built a four-cylinder car.

He worked as a designer for several companies, including Deutz at Cologne. While there, he is reputed to have designed and built in the cellar of his home a small car with a 1208cc eight-valve four-cylinder engine with shaft drive. This was to form the basis of the cars he

Below: The Bugatti Brescia (Type 22) was made until 1926 and had a 1386cc 16-valve engine. The name came from its success in the 1921 Brescia Grand Prix in northern Italy.

*Left: 1327cc Type 13, built around 1913
Right: A British-owned 1925 Brescia
model*

manufactured in 1910 after leaving the company.

Five 1327cc-engined Bugattis were made that year at his premises in Molsheim, Alsace, but the number rose to 75 the following year. Bugatti built a smaller 855cc-engined car in 1911 and Peugeot took it up and called it the Bébé Peugeot, making no less than 3,095 examples.

Bugatti's partner Ernst Friderich began racing Bugattis and won his class in the 1911 Grand Prix de France.

Bugatti built a five-litre car in 1913 – which had three valves per cylinder – two inlet and one exhaust. Only seven were made but they paved the way for the three-valve Type 30 and Type 37 engines which were to come in the 1920s. The smaller Type 13, as it was known, continued to be produced until World War I.

Alsace was a province of Germany until 1918 and Bugatti's premises were turned over to the war effort. Bugatti himself spent the war years in Paris where he was responsible for the design of aero-engines, including the 16-cylinder double-bank 500bhp engine made by the Duesenberg Motors Corporation of Elizabeth, New Jersey.

Molsheim became French territory at the end of World War I and Bugatti returned and resumed production of the Type 13. Its successor was a 16-valve model which was later called the Brescia after Friderich's win in the 1921 Grand Prix de Voiturettes at Brescia in northern Italy.

The car was an immediate success and about 2000 were made until 1926, many built under licence in other countries.

Bugatti entered the more exclusive end of the market with the Type 30 in 1922. It had a two-litre straight-eight engine. The later Type 35 had the rare distinction of being capable of winning Grands Prix and also being available for sale to amateurs. Between the wars it was the most

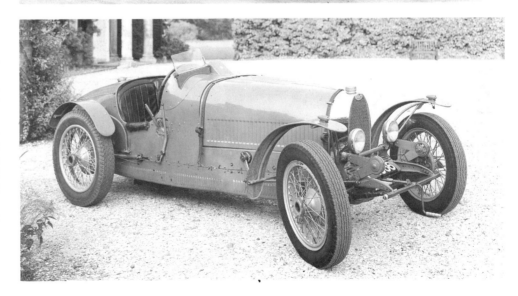

*Above right: Type 35B, a very successful
racer
Right: 1925 1.5-litre Type 37*

successful racing car available, winning 12 major Grands Prix in 1926.

The 1½-litre Type 37 was available for those not wealthy enough to buy a Type 35, and the Type 40 was affectionately dubbed Ettore's Morris Cowley because of its relatively modest performance and reasonable price.

Bugatti had dreamed of making the ultimate car to beat the world as far back as 1913. His dream came true with the Type 41 Royale in 1926. With a 15-litre engine and a claimed 300bhp it was a sensational car in its day, but only six were made and just three were sold. The rest remained with Bugatti's family.

Bugatti later concentrated on building

Above: 1927 2.3-litre Type 43
Left: Kellner-bodied Type 41 "Royale"

property speculations seriously hit Bugatti's finances and he moved to Paris to design aircraft and boats, leaving his son Jean in charge at Molsheim.

Jean was principally responsible for the last serious production Bugatti – the 3.3-litre double-overhead-camshaft straight-eight Type 57 which was introduced in 1934. By 1939, a total of 683 had been made. Jean was killed test-driving a racing car near Molsheim in August 1939, just

high-speed rail-cars, with the first going into production in 1933.

The Depression, the price of his straight-eight cars and a number of bad

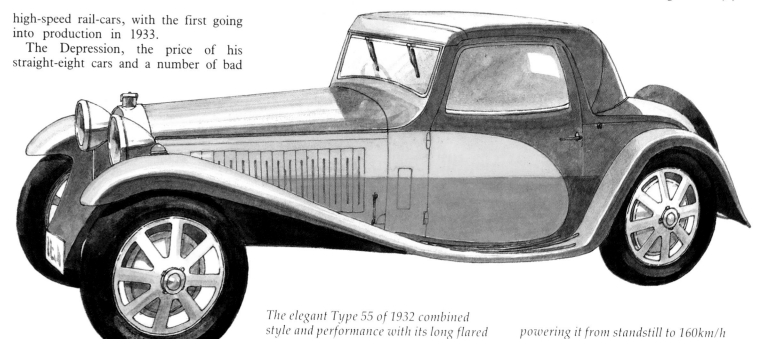

The elegant Type 55 of 1932 combined style and performance with its long flared wings and cutaway sides. Its eight-cylinder, 2.3-litre engine was capable of powering it from standstill to 160km/h (100mph) in 43 seconds and on to a top speed of 185km/h (115mph).

before the outbreak of World War II.

Molsheim once again had to contribute to the war effort. Bugatti moved to Bordeaux and worked on a number of projects. With the help of his younger son Roland he produced the 1½-litre Type 73, although few had been made by the time of his death in August 1947.

Above: Eight-cylinder, 200bhp Type 50T

Below left: 1952 supercharged Type 101C

An updated Type 57 went into production at Molsheim in 1951 under the direction of Pierre Marco, but only about 20 left the factory.

Further attempts to keep the company alive failed and it was bought by Hispano-Suiza in 1963, later being absorbed by S.N.E.C.M.A., the nationalized French aerospace conglomerate. Production at Molsheim was switched to the manufacture of aircraft parts.

Fearing that it might eventually be devalued as a 'designer' label, in 1987 a group of European businessmen acquired rights to the Bugatti name. Only afterwards, they claim, did they have the idea of reviving the marque. From a brand-new factory in Campogalliano, Italy, Bugatti Automobili SpA. intends to introduce a 322km/h (200mph) supercar, all-wheel-driven by a 550bhp 3.5-litre quad-turbo V12, in the early 1990s.

Bugatti Automobili

Italy
1987-1994

The rebirth of Bugatti was much welcomed when Bugatti Automobili SpA was founded in Modena in 1987. New owner, Romano Artioli, soon set about building a factory and quickly revealed that the first of the new Bugattis would have four-wheel-drive and a brand-new V12 engine. The new car, the EB110 GT was not launched until three years later, in 1991, the first car being delivered to its buyer the following year.

It was a car that went straight to the top of the supercar league, and was much praised by the motoring press. Everything seemed to be going well and the factory was soon promising to deliver a further 150 cars in 1993, although by the end of the year it was announced that only 98 had been built. However, in the same year, a stunning new model, the EB112 saloon, designed by and to be built by ItalDesign, was revealed at the 1993 Geneva show. Also in 1993 Bugatti bought Lotus for a rumoured £30 million, building Elans from the leftover components.

But by 1994 the rot had set in and Bugatti began to descend down the slippery slope towards bankruptcy: Artioli's promised production levels had once again not been reached, and ItalDesign stopped work on the EB112, citing lack of payment. Finally, after months of rumoured buyouts, several failed rescue attempts, and many court hearings, the end came. Bugatti Automobili SpA was declared bankrupt.: the company never disclosed any production or sales figures. The actual number built will probably never be known, such was the secrecy behind this fantastic supercar. Thankfully, Lotus was not brought down with Bugatti and was rescued by the Malaysian company, Proton.

Below: Bugatti boss, Romano Artioli's sense of tradition was tremendously strong and the standard EB110 was painted in unmistakable Bugatti blue. This was traditional but the construction was not. The EB110 used a carbonfibre monocoque designed by the French company, Aérospatiale

Right: This silver car, shown outside the Bugatti factory is an EB110S, the sports-racing version of the EB110. It was stripped for lightness, had an extra 40bhp and a fixed rear wing, unlike the standard car whose rear wing rose automatically at speed

Buick

U.S.A.
1903 to date

David Dunbar Buick formed the Buick Motor Company in 1903, but the company had a hesitant start and production proper did not get under way until 1904. Buick was poorly financed and had little in the way of future plans until William C. Durant bought it that year as his first car venture. Durant reorganized Buick for greater production and bought it a new factory. The 1905 Model 'C' became a great success and, by 1907, Buick was second only to Ford in U.S. sales. Nearly 14,000 cars had been built by the time Durant made the marque the cornerstone of his General Motors empire in 1908.

Buick's success weathered G.M.'s financial problems of 1910, and that year's sales figures outstripped those of every other manufacturer worldwide. There-

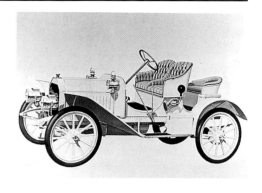

Above: 1905 Model C with 20bhp flat-twin
Below: 1908 Model 10 runabout

Above: Rakish lines of 1908 runabout
Below: A typical 1912 Buick tourer

Below: Buick's first six-cylinder car arrived in 1914, but the 1924 models, such as this Six, were distinguished by a Packard-like radiator and the company's first four-wheel brakes.

Above: Four-cylinder 1912 model Buick
Below: 1927 six-cylinder Buick

Above: 1914 B-55, the first six-cylinder
Below: 1932 Series 80 four-door sedan

Above: 1925 Standard Six
Below centre: 1937 convertible model 80C

after, Buick would always figure among the best-sellers. Delco electric lighting and starting were standard by 1914, when Buick marketed its first six-cylinder model, and it would be the six-cylinder range which would be the marque's sales strength throughout the 1920s, although there were four-cylinder models on offer as well.

An overhead-valve straight-eight was introduced in 1931 for all models, but Buick's evolution in the 1930s was dictated largely by General Motors policy. Thus, synchromesh gearboxes became standard in 1932, a cruciform-braced frame and no-draught ventilation arrived in 1933, 'knee-action' independent front suspension came in 1934, and turret-top styling, downdraught carburation and hydraulic brakes in 1936. Top of the range were the Roadmaster and Limited models, though the Century range of 1935–1942 put the biggest engine into a lighter and smaller package to give sparkling performance.

After World War II, straight-eight production was resumed, but 1948 saw changes with the arrival of two-speed Dynaflow automatic transmission and G.M.'s first 'hard-top' body in the shape of the Roadmaster Riviera. After 1953, the straight-eight remained for only a year

longer in the cheaper Special range, while the Super and Roadmaster models had the marque's first V8, a 188bhp overhead-valve design which was standardized

across the range in 1954. Between then and 1957, the high-performance Buicks were the Century range, which featured ever more powerful variants of that V8 engine.

Below: 1949 Model 71 Roadmaster

Below: 1948 Series 50 Eight Super

The Buicks of 1957 were heavier and slower, and sales dropped in 1958. In common with other G.M. marques, the 1961 models were down-sized to include a new all-aluminium 215-cubic inch V8 of 155bhp in the compact Special. But the demand for 'muscle cars' ensured the survival of the big V8s in models like the 1963 Riviera sports coupé. By 1966, Buick

Above: 1963 Buick Electra
Below: 1963 325bhp Riviera hardtop

Above: 'Compact' 1963 Special Wagon
Below: 1968 Wildcat custom hardtop coupé

had an altogether more sporting image, with V6 or small-block V8 engines in its smaller cars, while large V8s continued in the bigger models. Engine capacities continued to rise until the end of the decade, but the Buicks of the 1970s and 1980s began to lose their individuality as G.M. marques began to share more and more components.

The accent was now on fuel economy, not performance. Catalytic converters were standardized across the range in 1975 to meet the new U.S. exhaust emissions

Below: This 1934 model convertible Buick had an overhead-valve straight-eight engine of 278 cubic inches, giving 100bhp. Front suspension was General Motors' new 'knee-action' type, designed by Maurice Olley.

Above: 1973 Century Luxus coupé

Above: 1975 Electra Park Avenue (left) and V6 Skyhawk sub-compact (right)

Above: 1978 V6 Century Limited saloon

laws, and engines became smaller: a V6 became available again, though big V8s remained available until 1981. The first diesel-powered Buick arrived in 1980, and even four-cylinder engines were available in the cheapest Skylark, which was little more than a badge-engineered Chevrolet. As the cars became smaller, so did Buick's sales figures – between 1984 and 1988, those almost halved. Managers of the marque finally realized Buicks should seek to regain their traditional, opulent character, quite distinct from Oldsmobiles and Chevrolets.

Below: 1980 turbocharged Regal Sport
Bottom: 1980 Skyhawk with V6 engine

Above: 1980 Le Sabre sedan
Below: 1990 Reatta convertible

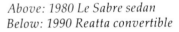

Left: The stunning Buick Riviera coupé was available with a supercharged V6

Above: The 1998 Buick Park Avenue Ultra had a large amount of standard luxury features

Below: The Buick Skylark was face-lifted in 1991 and used four- and six-cylinder engines. The Skylark name dates back to 1953

By the late 1990s Buick was starting to regain its luxury image, but was still struggling to keep pace with the competition, especially the new luxury Japanese imports. Staying with the traditional Buick model names, the company set about modernizing its range. By 1997, all Buick models had front-wheel-drive and the large displacement V8s seemed to be gone for good.

The new range used transversely-mounted pushrod V6s, with capacities ranging from 3.1 to 3.8 litres. Performance models relied on supercharging rather than cubic inches for the extra power.

Perhaps the best-looking nineties Buick was the Riviera, which was restyled in 1993. It had ultra-modern coupé styling and its V6 engine was available in 208bhp or 243bhp supercharged forms. It was a long way from the 1963 original but was just as desirable and really helped place Buick near the top of the General Motors family tree. The Regal and Park Avenue were also available with the supercharged engine.

The 1997 Park Avenue Ultra was Buick's flagship. It was all-new and a bigger car than its predecessor. Buick's best seller in the nineties though, was the LeSabre. The company built on the car's success by sticking with a winning formula and only minor cosmetic changes were made.

Right: 1998 Buick Century Custom. By 1998 it was a long way removed from its 1981 ancestor, with modern styling and mechanicals

Above: Buick Regal LS

Below: Buick Le Sabre LTD

Index

Encyclopedia of cars   629.222
      Volume 1

MY 19 '98
  JE 17 '98
  JUL 29 '98
AG 24 '06
OC 04 07
JY 21 '08
MY 20 '09'

  AG 17 15